ISRAEL TODAY

ISRAEL TODAY

RICHARD WOLFF

TYNDALE HOUSE PUBLISHERS
Wheaton, Illinois

Coverdale House Publishers Ltd.
London, England

Distributed in Canada by
Home Evangel Books Ltd.
Toronto, Ontario

Library of Congress Catalog Card Number 77-123289
SBN 8423-1810-0

Printed in the United States of America

CONTENTS

THE MIDDLE EAST

One of the most popular stories in Israel is the one about a fish which was asked by a scorpion to take him on his back across the Jordan River. At first the fish refused. "You would," he said, "sting me."

"Why would I?" replied the scorpion. "You know I can't swim. If I stung you, I too would drown."

So the fish saw the point and agreed to carry the scorpion, but halfway across the scorpion stung him. "You fool," said the fish, "now we will both drown. Why did you do that?"

"Oh, I don't know," replied the scorpion; "this is the Middle East."

Almost everything about the Middle East is irrational — both beyond reason and utterly unreasonable. There is not even a universally accepted definition of what constitutes the Middle East. No one is sure of the Middle East boundaries. Countries are included or excluded depending on the viewpoint of the speaker. At its maximum the Middle East stretches from Morocco to East Pakistan, a distance of 6,250 miles from east to west. A more restricted view would include the area from the United Arab Republic to Iran. This would, at any rate, be the heartland of the Middle East.

The Middle East is a link between three continents: Eu-

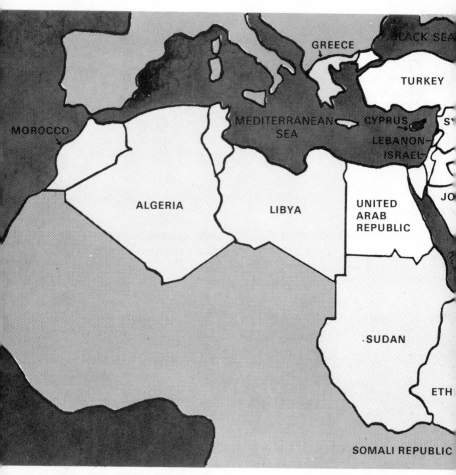

rope, Asia, and Africa. Here, three continents converge. The Mediterranean Sea, Persian Gulf, and Red Sea provide easy ingress deep into a land mass of gigantic proportions. "The juxtaposition of penetrating water areas separated by land bridges creates a geographical situation not found in like degree elsewhere in the world."[1]

The Middle East has been of immense importance from time immemorial. Some of the most ancient civilizations

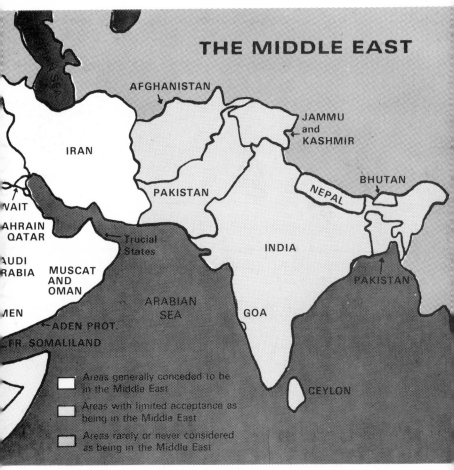

THE MIDDLE EAST

AFGHANISTAN

JAMMU and KASHMIR

IRAN

BHUTAN

PAKISTAN

NEPAL

VAIT

AHRAIN
QATAR

Trucial States

INDIA

AUDI
RABIA

MUSCAT AND OMAN

PAKISTAN

MEN

ARABIAN SEA

GOA

ADEN PROT.

FR. SOMALILAND

CEYLON

Areas generally conceded to be in the Middle East

Areas with limited acceptance as being in the Middle East

Areas rarely or never considered as being in the Middle East

originated in the "fertile crescent". Here great empires rose and fell including the Egyptian, Sumerian, Assyrian, Babylonian, Hittite, Persian, Macedonian, Roman, Byzantine, Abbasid, and Ottoman. Even today over 100 million people inhabit the Middle East — given the narrowest definition.

It is hardly necessary to remind anyone that the Middle East is the cradle of the three great monotheistic religions of the world: Judaism, Christianity, and Islam. Jerusalem and Mecca are centers of intense religious interest.

One might have expected that in our day of modern communications the strategic position of the Middle East would have been impaired. A new factor has come into play to enhance the world importance of the Middle East — oil. Over one-third of the world oil production comes from the Middle East. Western Europe, consuming almost twice as much oil as eastern Europe, the USSR, and China combined, depends largely on the Middle East for oil imports. As much as 80 percent of its oil supply comes from the Middle East. Naturally, most of the major oil-producing countries try to maintain good relations with the West. The Communist countries produce 17 percent and consume 15 percent of the world's oil, exporting 2 percent — they are therefore ruled out as a market for Middle Eastern oil.

There is more. Oil reserves in the Middle East seem to increase in millions of barrels with each new advance in geological exploration. About two-thirds of the world's oil reserves are in the Middle East. Excluding Libya and Algeria, at least 18 percent of the area's reserves are concentrated around the shores of the Persian Gulf. The strategic importance of the Middle East cannot be overrated.

It is not surprising that the great powers have always been involved in Middle East politics. American interest in the Middle East dates back to the early days of the Republic. Trading vessels made voyages to the eastern Mediterranean as far back as 1785. An American consul established offices in Smyrna in 1824. But despite oil interests and religious activities, the United States was not deeply involved in the Middle East till World War II. At that time growing Soviet pressure from the north and declining British power combined to create an imbalance in the Middle East. In 1955 with U.S. and U.K. support, Iran, Turkey, Pakistan, and Iraq signed the Baghdad Pact for mutual security and economic development. As might be expected, the pact was vigorously opposed by the USSR as well as Arab opponents of British influence in the Middle East. To counter the pact, the USSR and Egypt made an arms deal in 1955, a pattern which was soon followed by other Arab countries. Iraq withdrew from the Baghdad Pact and the Central Treaty Organization (CENTO) emerged as a new alliance in 1959. It was in 1958 that President Eisenhower responded to an appeal for help from the President of Lebanon and United States troops were landed to safeguard the independence of the country. U.S. involvement has gradually increased, both in terms of arms shipments into the area and concern over maritime rights, as well as the political and territorial integrity of all states in the region.

The USSR has always had a consuming interest in the Middle East, stemming partly from strategic considerations and partly from a desire to gain access to the Mediterranean. Literally for centuries Russia has sought to expand south toward the Black and Caspian seas in order to gain access to those seas and egress through the straits into the Mediterranean. This has provoked many historic conflicts between Russia and the Byzantine, Turkish, and British empires. The implementation of these age-old dreams began under Peter the Great, when the power of the Ottoman Empire began to wane. "Russia's Catherine the Great longed to acquire Turkish Constantinople and found there a new empire. Constantinople would have given Russia the port it wanted, as well as access through the Dardanelles and the Bosporous to the Mediterranean. In the Crimean War, the Czarist armies of Alexander were stopped just short of attaining Catherine's goal. Under Lenin and Stalin, the Communists seemed to lose interest in the Middle East. But after World War II, the traditional Russian attraction to the south began to assert itself once more."[2]

Control of the Black Sea was achieved after four wars with Turkey. The victory achieved in 1774 gave the Russians possession of the Crimea.

The violent history of the Middle East due to its strategic importance, the huge oil production and fantastic oil reserves, the keen interest of the superpowers, the many political coups and interminable intrigues, the creation of the state of Israel and the religious conflicts — all these ingredients combined to keep the Middle East a seething area of intense conflict, ready to erupt at the slightest provocation.

THE PROMISED LAND

If the boundaries of the Middle East are ill defined, it may come as a much greater surprise that the same holds true of the boundaries of the promised land.

Although the expression "the promised land" does not occur in the Old Testament, nor in the ancient rabbinical writings, the idea of the land is part and parcel of the call of Abraham. He "was called to go out to a place which he was to receive as an inheritance," and although at first "he went out not knowing where to go" (Heb. 11:8; Gen. 12:1), Canaan was soon pointed out as the land of promise (Gen. 12:7).

God specified that the land was given to Abraham and to his descendants forever (Gen. 13:15). The promise was reiterated from time to time (Gen. 17:8) and renewed to Isaac (Gen. 26:3) and Jacob (Gen. 28:13; 35:12).

The geographic limits were indicated for the first time in Gen. 15:18-21:

> "from the river of Egypt to the great river, the river Euphrates, the land of the Kenites, the Kenizzites, the Kadmonites, the Hittites, the Perizzites, the Rephaim, the Amorites, the Canaanites, the Girgashites and the Jebusites."

This text deserves careful analysis:

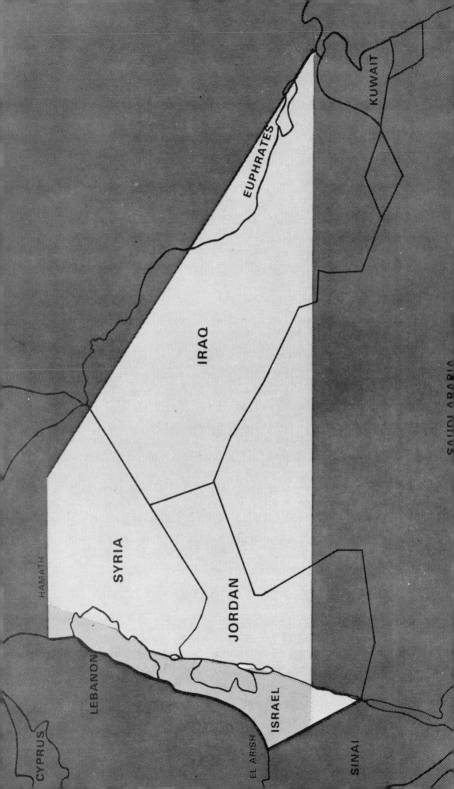

The *river of Egypt* is not the Nile, but El Arish, a river approximately in the northeast corner of the Sinai peninsula.

The *river Euphrates,* the largest river of western Asia, flows through ancient Mesopotamia into the Persian Gulf. The river traverses Iraq which it practically cuts in two and flows through Syria into Turkey.

Although the southwestern and eastern boundaries are clearly indicated, the northern and southern frontiers are not specified in this text. It is difficult to determine the exact territory of the ten nations which occupied the land.

In Numbers 34, the borders of the land of Canaan are more precisely defined, after the reminder that "this is the land that shall fall to you for an inheritance, the land of Canaan in its full extent" (v. 2).

South: a line runs from the southern tip of the Salt Sea (now called the Dead Sea) through Kadesh-barnea to the Brook of Egypt.

West: the coastline of the Great Sea, i.e., the Mediterranean, is the natural border.

North: the land extends all the way up to Hamath, the modern Hamah in Syria, north of Lebanon (directly east of Cyprus). The city is located on the river Orontes.

East: the border runs down to the shoulder of the sea of Chinnereth (the sea of Galilee), and follows the Jordan down to the Salt Sea.

The tribal boundaries as detailed in Joshua 15-19 follow essentially the same outline, without disregarding the tribes which had settled on the east side of the Jordan.

Different shorthand expressions are used in popular fashion to describe the land, such as

> —from the wilderness of Zin (south) to Hamath (north); Num. 13:21.
> —from the Brook of Egypt (southwest) to the river Euphrates (east); 2 Kgs. 24:7; Is. 27:12.
> —from Hamath (north) to the Brook of Egypt; 1 Kgs. 8:65, cf. also 2 Chron. 9:26; 1 Chron. 13:5 where

the Sihor is probably identical with El Arish or the
Brook of Egypt; 1 Kgs. 4:21.
—from Dan to Beersheba; Judg. 20:1; 1 Sam. 3:20;
2 Sam. 3:10; 17:11; 24:2, 15; I Kgs. 4:25.

These were undoubtedly the ideal limits of the land, seldom occupied by Israel in its entirety, except under the rule
of King David and Solomon (1 Chron. 13:5; 1 Kgs. 4:21).

There is a striking discrepancy between

—the limits indicated for the first time in Genesis 15
and detailed later, including all of modern Israel,
most of Lebanon, Jordan, Syria, and Iraq, and
—the boundaries specified in Numbers 34, limited
on the eastern side to the river Jordan!

Interestingly enough, the futuristic description furnished
by Ezekiel repeats the same well-known landmarks (Hamath,
the Great Sea, the Brook of Egypt, the Jordan), but limits
the eastern border of the land to the Jordan (not the Euphrates; Ezek. 47:15-20). Here again it is essential to distinguish the ideal and the promise from the historical realization and the final fulfillment.

Micah seems to foresee that in a future day "the boundary shall be far extended" (7:11; cf. KJV which translates "decree" instead of "boundary"; the context favors the
rendering "boundary" ?) perhaps to accommodate the huge
population influx (v. 12; cf. Zech. 10:10). The same thought
is echoed in Is. 33:17: "Your eyes will see the king in his
beauty; they will behold a land that stretches afar."

Genesis 15 mentions ten nations as occupying the land
of promise in the days of Abraham, but Deut. 7:1 names
only seven as forming an obstacle to the advance of Joshua
in the day when God would bring them into the land. This
has not escaped the attention of ancient Jewish scholars
whose comments are indeed interesting.

First of all, they speak normally of the "land of Israel,"
rather than the holy land (Zech. 2:12), or the promised

land (Heb. 11:9). Rabbi Gamaliel II (toward A.D. 90) defined the boundaries of Israel as reaching north to the city of Achzib, a city south of Tyre, in the southwest corner of Lebanon. He speaks of the river which could be the Orontes in northern Syria, or the Euphrates (Challa 4:8).

Elsewhere, in answer to the question: What is Israel and what is foreign territory, a rabbinical opinion is furnished, indicating that a line could be drawn from the mountains of Amana (straight north of Damascus, in the northeast border of Lebanon) to the Brook of Egypt (Tos. Challa 2:11).

Some Rabbis distinguished different territorial divisions and indicated that the area from Achzib (nine miles north of Acre) to the mountains of Amana (north of Damascus) had not been reoccupied after the Babylonian exile.

When Paul spoke of the "seven nations in the land of Canaan" (Acts 13:19) he referred to Deut. 7:1 or Josh. 3:10 and 24:11 (the lists are identical). Elsewhere only six nations are mentioned, the Girgashites have been omitted (Ex. 3:8, 17; 23:23; 33:2; Deut. 20:17). At other times only five nations are mentioned (Ex. 13:5), sometimes only two (Gen. 13:7) and occasionally they are all included in the common name of Canaanites (Gen. 12:6).

These differences have taxed the ingenuity of the earliest Jewish scholars. God had promised the territory of ten nations (Gen. 15), but frequently only seven are mentioned (Deut. 7). R. Chelbo (A.D. 300) declared in the name of R. Jochanan († 279): Your fathers occupied the land of seven nations but in the days of the Messiah you will occupy the territory of ten nations. The three mentioned in Genesis 15 and omitted in Deuteronomy 7 are the Kenites, the Kenizzites, and the Kadmonites. According to R. Juda (A.D. 150) they represented Arabia, an Arabic tribe in Mesopotamia, and the Nabataeans. Most of the Rabbis decided, however, in favor of Edom, Moab, and Ammon. This opinion was based on the following interpretations:

> —Deut. 2:5 which definitely stated that the land of Edom was not to be part of Israel: "I will not give

you any of their land, no, not so much as for the
sole of the foot to tread on, because I have given
Mount Seir to Esau as a possession."
—as to Moab, reference was made to Deut. 2:9: "And
the Lord said to me, Do not harass Moab or contend
with them in battle, for I will not give you any of
their land for a possession, because I have given Ar
to the sons of Lot for a possession." It was further
assumed that
—the Kenizzites descended from Kenaz, who in turn
was a descendant of Esau (Gen. 36:11);
—the Kenites were the ancestors of the Moabites, and
the Kadmonites of the Ammonites.

The conclusion was simple:

Kenizzites	=	Edom
Kenites	=	Moab
Kadmonites	=	Ammon

There are some rabbis who concluded that the territory
of these three tribes, mentioned in Genesis 15 was not included in the promised land, a thought confirmed by Deut.
2:5, 9 — at least not "in this world," but only in the days of
Messiah. Indeed, even as it is written: "They shall put forth
their hand against Edom and Moab and the Ammonites
shall obey them" (Is. 11:14b). Cf. also Ps. 60:9; Obd. 19,
21 (among other Jewish sources notice Shebiith 6,36b, 46;
Gen. Rabba 64, etc.).

Regardless of debates concerning the present and future
extension of the land, a deep attachment to Israel underlies
all the discussions. R. Eleazar (A.D. 270) said: Any man
who owns no land is not a proper man; for it is said, The
heavens are the heavens of the Lord; but the earth he has
given to the children of men (Ps. 115:16). Since earth or
land are often translations of the same Hebrew word, Rabbi
Eleazar insisted that he who owned no land did not truly
belong to the children of men (Yebamoth 63a, 22).

Obviously, different conclusions are possible regarding the boundaries of the promised land. Whether the Jordan or the Euphrates forms the eastern border makes a tremendous difference. If the latter view is taken seriously by Jewish leaders today, it would threaten all of Jordan, and much of Syria and Iraq. Different Jewish positions are possible:

—the territory reaching to the Euphrates is included in the ancient promise, i.e., most of modern Jordan, Iraq, and parts of Syria should become an integral part of Israel. The northern frontier should include almost all of Lebanon. The land belongs to Israel by virtue of the promise and should become part of Israel as soon as possible.

—the borderline is formed by the river Jordan. The kingdoms of Jordan, Iraq, and Syria are excluded from the boundaries of the promised land. The northern frontier, however, includes most of Lebanon.

—ultimately, in the days of Messiah, Israel will reach to the Euphrates, but not before his coming. Meanwhile the northern limits should include Lebanon, whereas the Jordan forms the eastern frontier.

Aside from these possible religious views, the pragmatic politician — who may or may not quote the Old Testament Scriptures — may be satisfied with the status quo (or hope for more) and disregard the promise in favor of political reality. This tendency probably dominates national thinking.

The dilemma is obvious:

—if the promise is taken seriously, the frontiers should be expanded — *at least* to the north, since general agreement reigns regarding the northern border which reaches to the vicinity of Hamath.

—if the promise is disregarded, the "right to the land" might be questioned.

Is there a Christian view? As might be suspected, there is more than one:

> —Many Christians feel that the ancient promises regarding the land have no further significance, because Abraham himself "looked forward to the city which has foundations, whose builder and maker is God" (Heb. 11:10). His primary interest was spiritual, not material. Admittedly, God promised the land "forever" (Gen. 13:15), but it is pointed out that the word is used over 440 times in the Old Testament and often has a purely temporal meaning. For instance, the priesthood of Aaron was to last "forever" although it was ultimately replaced by the priest after the order of Melchizedek, i.e., Jesus Christ. Again, a slave might decide to remain in the household "forever," i.e., for a lifetime (Deut. 15:17b). Obviously, the meaning of the word "forever" is largely determined by the context.

But the main emphasis of the argument falls on the fact that the land was only a type and that the fulfillment has taken place in the church. Believers are the seed of Abraham (Gal. 3). Those who share his faith are his descendants (Rom. 4:16) and to Abraham and to his descendants it was promised "that they should inherit the world" (Rom. 4:13). The reference, so the argument goes, is obviously to Gen. 12:3, since there is no explicit passage in the Old Testament promising "the world" to Abraham. In his seed all nations are blessed (Gen. 12:3), a promise fulfilled in Christ (Acts 3:25, 26; Gal. 3:8). In other words, land (Gen. 12) = world (Rom. 4) and world = all nations — blessed through Christ. The promise is real, the blessing is in Christ. Christians who hold these views and take an amillennarian position feel that the return of Israel to the land has no biblical significance. It goes almost without saying that an element of truth has been retained in this exegesis which is easily overlooked. At the same time a future role of Israel is so clearly indicated (Rom. 11 et al.) that this exegesis is not altogether satisfactory.

> —There is another school of thought which takes the promise regarding the land quite literally (sometimes disregarding the valuable insight of the other position). Throughout history these Christian believers taught that one day Israel would return to the land. In fact, "the interest in the return of the Jews to Palestine was kept alive in the first part of the nineteenth century more by Christian millennarians, especially in Great Britain, than by Jews themselves" (*Encycl. Brit.* art. Zionism). Naturally, modern expositors were confirmed in their views when events converged to justify a position which had been advocated for generations regardless of seemingly adverse political circumstances. This view had been based on the literal interpretation of a large number of Scripture passages such as Is. 11: 11, 12; Jer. 24:6; Ezek. 36:24-28; Joel 3:20; Amos 9:14, 15; Zech. 10:8 ff.

As to the promise that Abraham and his descendants "should inherit the world" (Rom. 4:13), it is true that those who share the faith of Abraham are his spiritual descendants (Rom. 4:16), but the world they are to inherit should not be identified with the reception of all nations into the kingdom of God. If we are children, then we are heirs with Christ and his inheritance is the world to come, the new heaven and the new earth in which righteousness dwells (Rom. 8:17; 2 Pet. 3:13; cf. Dan. 7:27; Mt. 5:5). The fact that the land promised to Abraham may be typical of this ultimate possession does not nullify the reality of the promise concerning the land of Israel.

Granted the validity of this premillennarian concept, the question regarding the boundaries of Israel is not automatically solved. How much does it take to fulfill God's ancient promise? Must Israel occupy all the land to the Euphrates? Or to the Jordan? Or most of Lebanon? Must this occur before or after the coming of the Messiah? Could guidelines be found in previous historic events?

The Babylonian captivity of Israel had been predicted by Jeremiah to last for seventy years (Jer. 25:12). Although only about fifty thousand Jews returned to the land after the Babylonian captivity, the promise of God had been fulfilled! Only a fraction of those who had been deported and were multiplied in exile under God's blessing, returned to the land of promise — yet God's word was literally fulfilled (Ezra 1:1). The land area occupied by the returning Jews was minimal compared to the pre-exilic boundaries. It has been estimated that at first only Jerusalem and the immediate vicinity of the capital belonged to Israel. The territory occupied by the returning exiles stretched perhaps no more than twenty-five miles in a straight line. In fact, the Persians retained the overlordship and Israel was not totally independent.

Reading the prophecies concerning the return, one might have expected a far more glorious restoration. Nevertheless, the word of God was definitely fulfilled, although some people were seriously disappointed (Ezra 3:12; Hag. 2:3).

Could the same principles be in operation for the second recovery (Is. 11:11) which has now begun? Is the word of God sufficiently fulfilled both in terms of population (only 50,000 returned after the Babylonian exile) and land (only a few square miles were occupied by the Jews after the previous exile)? Are God's ancient promises fulfilled by virtue of the fact that the nation has been reestablished, regardless of boundaries or population? Could it be that the prophecies are "overfulfilled"? Will the remaining prophecies be fulfilled with the advent of Christ?

There are, then, at least three different Christian positions:

> —the current return to the land has no spiritual meaning.

—the return is a literal fulfillment of God's promises:
(a) all the land (to the Jordan or Euphrates) must be occupied and all the Jews return to Israel as soon as possible.
(b) a sufficient land area has been occupied already to satisfy a literal interpretation and fulfillment of the divine promises. Enough people may have returned already (or too many?). With the coming of Christ the remaining promises will be fulfilled literally.

The last view permits the Christian to point to the divine fulfillment without automatic endorsement of every political move made by Israel, either to enlarge her borders or to attract more immigrants.

Perhaps this needs to be emphasized. Many Christians — because of the unique position of the chosen people — tend to side with Israel, regardless of events. Humanitarian concerns are overlooked (the Arab refugee problem); for once, nationalistic views become secondary (the interests of the United States); a true Christian perspective is not reached because the viewpoint is too prejudiced and narrow. Objective evaluation becomes almost impossible because of eschatological presuppositions. If the thoughts mentioned above are taken into consideration, then the Christian, regardless of his prophetic views, regains the freedom to evaluate, to uphold or condemn as he sees fit from a truly biblical perspective.

The word of God is not only concerned with Israel or the promised land. A nation does not exist in a vacuum and even as in the past the prophetic vision embraced many world empires and smaller nations surrounding Israel, so it is with regard to the future. It is therefore imperative to review the situation of the surrounding nations.

EGYPT

The history of Israel cannot be understood without frequent reference to the history of Egypt. It is perhaps symbolic that the very earliest recorded mention of Israel outside of the Scriptures occurs on a victory stele or stone pillar erected by the Egyptian King Marniptah about 1220 B.C. The ancient stele informs us: "The people of Israel is desolate; it has no offspring." At that time Israel had barely conquered part of Canaan. The Israeli occupation of Canaan led to collision with Egypt since western Palestine had been subject to Egyptian rule for centuries.

For the next thousand years of Israeli history Egypt is always seen in the background, occasionally casting a long shadow over Israel, threatening, conquering, controlling. Most significant, perhaps, was the invasion of Shishak shortly after the death of Solomon. A huge Egyptian host carried fire and sword over the country, devastating many cities. In the great Karnak list, Shishak mentioned more than 150 places which he claimed to have conquered.

At times Egypt was an unreliable ally and the foreign entanglement of Israel was often denounced by the prophets. Ezekiel's rueful analogy is striking: "Israel leaned on you but, like a cracked staff, you snapped beneath her hand

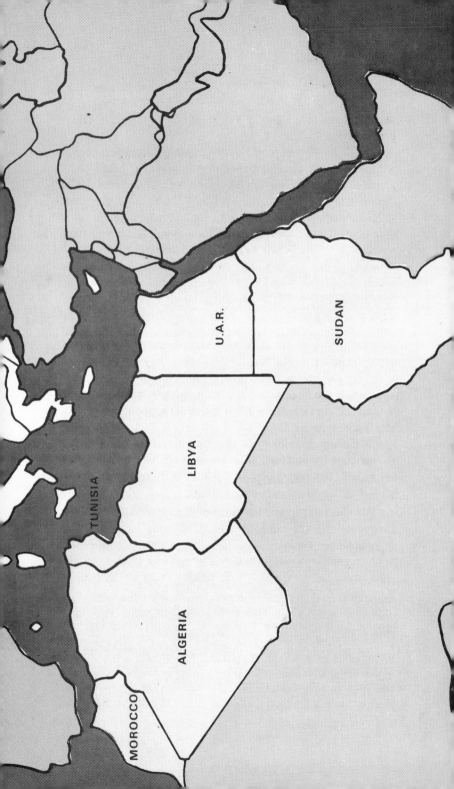

and wrenched her shoulder out of joint and made her stagger with pain" (Ezk. 29:7).

Egypt was not beyond the prophetic vision of the ancient seers. Jeremiah proclaimed that not only the kingdom of Judah, but all the surrounding nations would come under the control of the king of Babylon: "And now the Lord says this to evil nations, the nations surrounding the land that God gave his people Israel: See, I will force you from your land just as Judah will be forced from hers; but afterwards I will return and have compassion on all of you, and I will bring you home to your own land again, each man to his inheritance . . . Israel and her neighboring lands shall serve the king of Babylon for seventy years" (12:12, 14; 25:11). This announcement was fulfilled with striking accuracy.

Similarly, Ezekiel announced the downfall of Egypt: "For you have said, 'The Nile is mine; I have made it for myself!' . . . Therefore the Lord God said: 'I will bring an army against you, O Egypt, and destroy both men and herds. The land of Egypt shall become a desolate wasteland . . . I will utterly destroy the land of Egypt, from Migdol to Syene, as far south as the border of Ethiopia' " (chap. 29).

Ezekiel added that Egypt would be restored, that the Egyptians would return from banishment, but afterward Egypt would be an unimportant minor kingdom. "It shall be the most lowly of the kingdoms, and never again exalt itself above the nations; and I will make them so small that they will never again rule over the nations" (29:14).

"Historically this has been eminently true," comments F. Gardiner. "For a little while Egypt struggled against its oppressors, but its power was already broken, and from the time of its conquest by Cambyses it has never been for any length of time independent. There are few stronger contrasts in any inhabited country than between the ancient glory, dignity, power and wealth of Egypt, and its later insignificance."[3]

The prophetic announcement regarding the minor role

of Egypt is extraordinary. There was absolutely no reason to anticipate such a turn of events. The power of Babylon did not last much longer than the life of Nebuchadnezzar. One might have expected that Egypt, along with other nations, would once again enjoy freedom and rise to a place of eminence.

For one brief moment it did seem that the old Egyptian glory would return, but the power vacuum created by the decline of Babylon did not last. Persia emerged as a major power and the energetic Cambyses invaded Egypt in 525 B.C. In vain did Amasis, king of Egypt, endeavor to rescue the empire through an alliance with Greek mercenaries. His son, Psamtik III, could not stop the invaders and fell before the invading forces of Cyrus of Persia. Soon all of Egypt was occupied and became a Persian province.

The Persians controlled Egypt until they were succeeded by the Greeks under the leadership of Alexander the Great (332 B.C.).

In turn the Romans dispossessed the Greeks and became the new masters of Egypt. The Roman period lasted until the Muslim conquest. It took only a small army of 4,000 men followed by a second expeditionary corps of 12,000 men to subdue Egypt and defeat the Romans in A.D. 640. For the next 300 years Egypt was simply a province of the Eastern Caliphate.

The early caliphs were immediate successors of Mohammed and ruled Egypt from Medina in Arabia. A little later the capital was transferred north to Damascus and around A.D. 750 to Baghdad. Dynasties followed each other with varying degrees of independence, among them the famous Mamelukes. True independence was never regained as Egypt stood always in relationship to the Caliphate.

In 1517 Egypt became part of the Ottoman Empire, governed from Constantinople. Napoleon's Syrian campaign led to French occupation of Egypt, and British occupation brings us to modern times. It was in 1914 that Egypt became a British protectorate, which was terminated in 1921 when Egypt was declared independent.[4]

The Sultan assumed the title of king and proclaimed Egypt a monarchy. King Fuad was followed by his son Farouk who assumed royal responsibility at the age of seventeen.

This quick review bears out the remarkable prediction of Ezekiel, that although Egypt would be restored and not be annihilated as some of the other nations which disappeared in the night of history, the nation would never again be a significant world power. This does not mean that Egypt could not defeat Israel or lead an Arab coalition. But the position once occupied by Egypt was similar to the one now enjoyed by the "Big Two" of the atomic era, and that has been lost irrevocably.

Before the outbreak of World War II Egypt hosted the pan-Arab congress which met to consider the Arab case in Palestine. After the danger of a German invasion was removed, renewed attention was concentrated on the Palestine problem. It was almost to be expected that Egyptian troops would enter Gaza on May 16, 1948, following the Israeli declaration of independence. Initial success was followed by military reversals and on February 24, 1949, an armistice was signed between Egypt and Israel. Gaza remained in Egyptian hands.

The coup of January 25, 1952, altered Egyptian politics fundamentally. King Farouk was compelled to abdicate. General Naguib declared Egypt a republic, and military officers ruled Egypt. One of the main reasons for public deep-seated dissatisfaction was the humiliating debacle suffered in the first Palestinian war. The problem of the Sudan and Anglo-Egyptian relations was another source of friction.

On April 18, 1954, Colonel Nasser became Premier. He was the only candidate in the elections of June 1956 and was elected President. In October of that year Israel launched an offensive against Egypt, coordinated with an Anglo-French attack. An armistice was signed in early November. The result of the Suez conflict was an enormous increase in prestige for Nasser. He had nationalized the Canal, resisted Western pressure, and survived the combined attack of three nations. A union with Syria was proclaimed on February 1, 1958, and the United Arab Republic (UAR) came into being. The union lasted until 1961 when Syria seceded. Nasser intensified his social revolution which led to repeated collision with Saudi Arabia, Jordan, and Yemen. During 1964 relations with all Arab countries (with the single exception of Syria) improved. The first stage of the Aswan Dam was completed with Russian help. Foreign relations were involved and far reaching, including Yemen, the Congo, North Africa, and complex international relations with the Western powers and the Eastern bloc.

Across the years Egypt's relationships with surrounding Arab nations underwent many changes and varied from extreme hostility to intimate brotherhood, depending on the prevailing political climate.

The year 1967 was crucial for Egypt, leading almost to total disaster. Although Israel had declared that the closing of the Gulf of Aqaba would be an act of war, Nasser claimed sovereignty over the Gulf on May 22. The Six-Day War followed. The outcome is well known. Nasser's resignation followed on June 9 and caused consternation. Public demonstration followed and Nasser withdrew his resignation the next day. He assumed full responsibility for the events leading up to the June War and for the "grave setback."

Egyptian losses were indeed extremely high. In the Sinai tank battle 325 Israeli tanks opposed 850 Egyptian tanks — it was the largest tank battle in history. Egypt lost an enormous amount of war matériel and suffered heavy casualties. As many as 10,000 soldiers and 1,500 officers were killed and 5,500 officers and enlisted men (including four generals) were taken prisoner. They were ultimately exchanged for nine Israelis. As much as 80 percent of Egypt's military equipment was lost.

The economic situation was depressing. The closure of

the Suez Canal seriously cut into Egyptian revenues. Tourist income dropped to an extremely low level. The result of the Khartoum Conference (August 29-Sept. 1, 1967) was a firm promise of approximately $270,000,000 aid from Saudi Arabia, Kuwait, and Libya, enabling Egypt to survive the loss of the income from the Suez Canal. The economy situation improved in 1968, especially in the realm of agriculture which developed to the point of export. Sufficient oil is now produced in Egypt to meet national demands. It is not easy to maintain a growing economy in the face of a population increase of almost one million per year.

In 1966 the Suez Canal handled an average of fifty-seven ships a day. The economic repercussions of the closure have been felt around the world. It is estimated that European countries lost one billion dollars because of the increased cost of sending oil tankers around Africa. Export of iron ore from India to Europe is no longer profitable. Egypt loses some $250,000,000 in yearly revenues or 25 percent of its foreign earnings.

At the Khartoum Conference Kuwait, Saudi Arabia, and Libya promised to hand out some $154,000,000, $140,-000,000, and $84,000,000 each year to both Egypt and Jordan "until the effects of aggression are eliminated." Of the total, about $270,000,000 was reserved for Egypt to compensate for the loss of revenue previously derived from the Suez Canal. Jordan received over $110,000,000 and an additional $14,000,000 was designated to help the Syrians (who boycotted the conference).

As long as the present situation continues, all talk of re-opening of the Canal is pointless. It is possible that the USSR would like to use the Canal to move into the Red Sea, the Persian Gulf, and the Indian Ocean. Egypt would undoubtedly enjoy the revenue. On the other hand, Egypt may also live with the fond hope that the maritime nations will put pressure on Israel to withdraw from the East Bank so that the Canal can be reopened. The United States is happy to see Soviet ships bound for North Vietnam go around the coast of Africa, traveling 14,000 miles instead of 7,000. Under the circumstances not much change can be expected in that particular area.

The UAR maintains that it stands by the November 22, 1967, resolution of the United Nations Security Council. This resolution called for a settlement based on Israeli withdrawal and the termination of the state of belligerency as well as for the right to free passage for Israeli ships through the international waterways. (See Appendix for the full text.)

Currently Egypt maintains 500,000 men under arms and a war chest of over one billion dollars. Several thousand Russian military and technical experts are active in Egypt. In the vital area of spare parts Egypt is entirely at the mercy of her Soviet partners. The effort to overcome this handicap by building Egyptian aircraft has failed. Two prototypes of the HA-300 have been built but the power plant has been a complete failure. The subsonic HA-300 is scarcely worth its metal. Their rockets have proved ineffective because they are without reliable guidance systems.

In terms of sheer numbers, the Egyptian army is formidable and has all the necessary modern equipment. With typical Arab rhetoric Nasser exhorts his people to fight against Israel "a battle of destiny on a sea of blood under a blazing sky." Practically every day news media report artillery duels, air strikes, raids, and armed clashes along the Suez Canal, separating Israeli and Egyptian forces.

As early as November 24, 1967, as he addressed the fifth session of the National Assembly, Nasser declared that the UAR was militarily stronger than in the days preceding the June war. Shortly afterwards, in his second speech to the nation since the end of the war, he declared: "What was taken away by force cannot be recovered except by force . . . we are committed to four principles: no recognition of Israel, no peace with Israel, no negotiations with Israel, and no interference in the Palestine issue which is a legitimate problem of the Palestinian people."

To some extent Nasser may be under pressure to maintain verbal and military attacks regardless of cost . . . and they are high.

> —for one thing Nasser must appease the zealous army officers, humiliated by repeated defeats. They are impatient for revenge and anxious to fight Israel;
>
> —Nasser needs to demonstrate his independence vis à vis the USSR. If the Russians advise caution, Nasser must demonstrate his authority by ordering an attack;
>
> —the fedayeen activity puts pressure on Nasser. He cannot allow the fedayeen to capture the headlines and expect to remain the key political leader;
>
> —Egyptian military activity would discourage any peace moves which might be initiated unilaterally by Jordan;
>
> —the frequent attacks maintain tension and guarantee continued involvement of the big powers;
>
> —the outward clashes divert attention from internal problems.

In order to understand Nasser it is essential to read his political testament which began as a series of three articles published in 1953 under the title *The Philosophy of the Revolution.* Nasser wrote them in cooperation with his confidant Mohamed Hassanein Heikal, editor of *Al Akbar.* By 1959 a million copies had been distributed. It became the Bible of the Nasser revolution. In the book Nasser traces the first elements of his Arab consciousness to the days when he was a student in a secondary school and went out on strike on December 2 every year as a protest against the Balfour Declaration. "When I asked myself at that time why I left my school enthusiastically and why I was angry for this land which I never saw, I could not find an answer except the echoes of sentiment."[5]

Nasser, inspired by the well-known story of Pirandello called "Six Characters in Search of an Author" writes: "The annals of history are full of heroes who carved for themselves great and heroic roles and played them on momentous occasions on the stage. History is also charged with great heroic roles which do not find actors to play them on the stage. I do not know why I always imagine that in this region in which we live there is a role wandering aimlessly about seeking an actor to play it. I do not know why this role, tired of roaming about in this vast region which extends to every place around us, should at last settle down, weary and worn out, on our frontiers beckoning us to move, to dress up for it and to perform it since there is nobody else who can do so."

The reference to "this vast region which extends to every place around us" was more narrowly defined as consisting of three specific circles. First of all there is the Arab circle, "the most important and the most closely connected with us. Its history merges with ours. We have suffered the same hardships, lived the same crises . . . religion also fused this circle with us . . . this circle is as much a part of us as we are a part of it . . . our history has been mixed with it and its interests are linked with ours. These are actual facts and not mere words."

Speaking of the first circle, Nasser adds that "none of its component parts could be isolated from the other; none could be as independent as an island, unconnected with the other parts. Such is the first circle in which we must revolve and attempt to move in as much as we possibly can. It is the Arab circle."

He then directs the attention of the reader to "the second circle, the circle of the continent of Africa" because it is impossible for Egypt to stand aside, "away from the sanguinary and dreadful struggle now raging in the heart of Africa between five million whites and two hundred million Africans." He emphasizes the fact that Egypt must be involved for one principal and clear reason, namely that Egypt is in Africa. The people of Africa will continue to look to Egypt, the country guarding the northern gate of the continent and constituting a connecting link with the outside world. The struggle of Africa "will affect us whether we want it to or not."

Finally there is a third circle, the broad Muslim world "with which we are tied by bonds which are not only forged by religious faith but also tightened by the facts of history."

This is the clear vision of President Nasser. Israel is an obstacle to the realization of this plan. Its geographic position seems to hinder the realization of the first circle and disturbs the broad circle of Muslim unity. Repercussions of the Israeli problem have even been felt across Africa, especially North Africa and the Sudan. To Nasser, Israel is the result of imperialism. If Palestine had not come under the British mandate, Zionism could not have succeeded and Israel would not have come into existence. To some extent, the formal recognition of Israel would be a denial of Nasser's political testament. On the other hand subservience to the USSR would also annihilate the preeminent rule of Egypt. First and foremost, Nasser is a nationalist, deeply concerned about the UAR — a charismatic leader who would like to see deep changes in the Arab nations to bring them into contemporary realities. He feels that the most potent weapon for change is a socialist revolution à la UAR style. This economic transformation coupled with linguistic unity and religious ties would be the necessary basis for the fulfillment of the first dream which would in turn give Egypt hegemony over vast areas of Africa and allow Egypt as the center of the first circle to play a dominant role in Muslim and Islamic affairs ranging from Indonesia to Morocco.

It comes as a total surprise, almost a shock, to discover that the last word concerning Egypt, the hereditary enemy, is not one of doom but of blessing. Again and again, the solemn refrain "in that day" is heard in Isaiah 19, spelling out the ultimate salvation of Egypt:

> In that day there will be an altar to the Lord in the midst of the land of Egypt, and a pillar to the Lord at

its border. It will be a sign and a witness to the Lord of hosts in the land of Egypt; when they cry to the Lord because of oppressors he will send them a savior, and will defend and deliver them. And the Lord will make himself known to the Egyptians; and the Egyptians will know the Lord in that day and worship with sacrifice and burnt offering, and they will make vows to the Lord and perform them. And the Lord will smite Egypt, smiting and healing, and they will return to the Lord, and he will heed their supplications and heal them. In that day there will be a highway from Egypt to Assyria, and the Assyrian will come into Egypt, and the Egyptian into Assyria, and the Egyptians will worship with the Assyrians. In that day Israel will be the third with Egypt and Assyria, a blessing in the midst of the earth, whom the Lord of hosts has blessed, saying, "Blessed be Egypt my people, and Assyria the work of my hands, and Israel my heritage."

(Is. 19:19-25)

A few explanatory notes may be in order. The *five cities* (v. 18) represent either:

—a large number, since five is half of ten, and the latter often symbolic of completeness;
—or, an indefinite number, since five is so used in Is. 17:6 and 30:17.

The fact that the five cities speak the *language of Canaan* indicates their conversion to the true God (cf. Zeph. 3:9). They will *swear allegiance to the Lord,* i.e., worship him (Deut. 6:13; 10:20). The oath is an act of worship, implying an acknowledgment of God's existence, a recognition of his attributes of omnipresence, omniscience, justice, and power and an admission of accountability.

One city is called *Ir Ha-Heres,* translated city of destruction (KJV) or City of the Sun (RSV). The context favors the KJV. The character of the city is expressed by the name (Is. 1:26; 61:3b), and City of the Sun would hardly be fitting. The Egyptians will, in fact, no longer worship the sun. On, called Heliopolis (City of the Sun) by the Greeks, was a few miles northeast of modern Cairo. It was the center of the worship of Ra, the sun god. The Hebrew word translated destruction might be a pun on the word "sun" to indicate that sun worship with all its emblems will be destroyed (see Jer. 43:13).* The *altar* (v. 19) might be a memorial (not for sacrifice; cf. Josh. 22:26, 27). The *pillar* was similar to the ancient obelisks, bearing an inscription designating the sovereign of the land. The pillar to the Lord is a recognition of the Lordship of God over the area (Gen. 28:18 ff.), so that altar and pillar are *a sign and a witness to the Lord.*

God will send them a *savior.* This savior is not an ordinary human deliverer who would help his own nation by inflicting injury on the enemy. The result of his activity is spelled out in v. 23. The previous verse (v. 22) is only a recapitulation of previous events (vv. 16, 17) and the main point is that *the Egyptians will know the Lord.* Egypt and Assyria will join in the worship of God and Israel will be *a blessing in the midst of the earth,* finally fulfilling her calling to be God's witness (Is. 43:11, 12, 21). Egypt is now *my people,* a title which had been reserved for Israel, and similarly Assyria is *the work of my hands.* The *highway* which links the two ancient world powers is symbolic of the new relationship. United in the service of God, no longer antagonistic to each other, they form an alliance, and Israel — so often crushed between them — is the third partner.

What about the fulfillment? The reference is *not* to the worship of Jews in Egypt, but to the conversion of the Egyptians and Assyrians. This rules out any reference to:

---

*See the exhaustive note of S. R. Driver in *Hastings Bible Dictionary,* article Ir Ha-Heres. He favors "city of destruction."

—a possible temple erected by Jewish mercenaries in upper Egypt toward 525 B.C.;

—the famous temple built by Onias, c. 170-160 B.C., (destroyed in A.D. 73). Onias based his undertaking on the text of Isaiah and built the temple in the district of Heliopolis.

The flourishing church in Egypt (which developed soon after Pentecost; Acts 2:9-11) did not exhaust the prophetic word. There is "a future in which this prophecy shall anew powerfully manifest itself" (Hengstenberg's *Christology of the Old Testament,* II:146), or, as Plumptre puts it: "like other bright ideals of the future, it yet waits for its complete fulfillment" (in *Ellicott's Commentary*). Although Gleason Archer points to Onias' temple and to Alexander the Great (as the savior) he also recognizes that the spread of the gospel in those lands "is but a foregleam of that final and more lasting peace that will be established between East and West in the days of the Messiah" (*Wycliffe Bible Commentary,* in loco).

When Israel as a whole will come to Christ it will mean "life from the dead," a worldwide spiritual resurrection (Rom. 11:12, 15), the spread of the good news concerning the Redeemer to all nations and first and foremost to Egypt and Assyria (Iraq). Then the power of Mohammedanism will be fully broken and millions will receive Christ as Lord and Savior. Once the heartland of Islam has yielded to Christ, it is easy to see how the rest of the Muslim world would be affected and ready to embrace the gospel.

LIBYA

The Lubim or Libyans are infrequently mentioned in the Old Testament. The KJV usually transliterates *Lubim* except in Dan. 11:43, where Libyans is used. The RSV translates Libya. The word occurs only in 2 Chron. 12:3; 16:8; Nah. 3:9 and Dan. 11:43, always in conjunction with Egypt. The prophetic text of Daniel informs us that the antichrist will stretch out his hand over Egypt and the traditional allies of Egypt, including Libya, will be unable to escape his control but will be compelled to "follow in his train" (Dan. 11:42, 43).

Another Hebrew word, Put, is occasionally translated Libya in the KJV, and rightly so. This identification is as old as the LXX (c. 250 B.C.) and also found in the Vulgate. Josephus informs us that "Phut was the founder of Libya" and speaks of a river by the same name "in the country of the Moors" (Ant. I:6:2). This is confirmed by Pliny, who mentions a river Phut in Mauretania. The identification of Put with Libya is confirmed by archaeological evidence.

The words of Jeremiah against Put (46:9) were fulfilled in the invasion of Nebuchadnezzar. If at one time mercenaries from Put served in the army of Tyre (Ezek. 27:10), they were usually in league with Egypt (Ezek. 30:5; Nah. 3:

9). Put, or Libya, is mentioned in the famous prophecy of Ezekiel 38 (v. 5) as part of the hordes invading Israel.*

One of the most famous Libyan kings, known to many Bible readers, was Shishak. He founded the Libyan dynasty in Egypt, supported Jeroboam I of Israel, and invaded Palestine (1 Kgs. 14:25, 26).

If Lubim describes Libya in a narrow sense — the area immediately adjoining Egypt — Put designates the Libyans in a broader sense, covering all of North Africa as far as Mauritania.

It was only on November 21, 1949, that the United Nations decided that an independent sovereign state of Libya should be formed no later than January 1, 1952. Modern Libya roughly corresponds to the ancient area of Lubim; therefore, the translation "Libya" is quite justified. Libya was admitted to the Arab League on March 28, 1953.

> "It is of interest that *at the time of the end Egypt will be in alliance with Libya* and the Sudan. The ancient and traditional alliance of Egypt, Cush (Sudan), the Lubim or Libya, and Put (covering North Africa almost from Egypt to Mauritania) will exist once more. The present alignment of power is not accidental. The national independence of these nations and their common perspective certainly foreshadows the situation we can expect in the end according to the prophet Daniel."[6]

These words, penned in 1967, have received dramatic fulfillment. The regime of king Idris was ousted September 1, 1969, by Col. Muammar Mohammed Gaddafi. This revolution was not altogether unexpected. King Idris had tried to abdicate as far back as 1964, and the crown prince, Hassan Rida el Seunussi, did not wish to exercise leadership. Flanked by two socialist countries, Algeria and Egypt, the

---

*It is possible that in Is. 66:19 we should read Put rather than Pul; compare with the RSV. The change is already found in the LXX.

revolution in Libya was only a matter of time. The immediate international repercussions of the coup have been tremendous:

- —although discussion regarding foreign bases goes back to 1964, the British were immediately compelled to withdraw their 1,700 troops from their remaining bases at Eladem and Tobruk.
- —the $100 million Wheelus Air Force Base was the last major military foothold of the United States on the African continent. The base agreement was to expire in 1971. Evacuation of the 3,000 U.S. servicemen and 7,000 dependents has already been completed. It is possible that the Russians will use the base after the U.S. departure. "Russian navy planes already operate from Egyptian air fields, keeping elements of the United States 6th Fleet under continuous surveillance. Russian ships have access to port facilities at Alexandria and Port Said in Egypt, and Russian technicians are known to be training Algerian navy personnel at Mers el Kebir, the former French base near Oran, less than 300 miles from Gibraltar."[7]
- —the 150 Peace Corps workers (mostly teachers) have left Libya.
- —one of the first acts of the new regime was to declare its solidarity with the Arab world. Almost immediately after the coup, a gift of one million dollars was made to Palestinian commando organizations.
- —oil is the key word in Libya. At the end of 1969, income from oil royalties and taxes was running at an annual rate of $1.2 billion . . . for only 1,700,000 inhabitants — or approximately $700 per capita! Of the thirty-eight companies involved, twenty-four are American, producing 3,100,000 barrels a day. Since the closure of the Suez Canal in 1967, oil ex-

ports have doubled since Libyan oil lies closer to Europe (without the Suez Canal) than most Arabian oil. In spite of this enormous income, the economy has lagged under the new regime, probably due to Libyanization of foreign-owned banks, nationalization of private hospitals, a review of all building projects (temporarily suspended) and similar measures. The economic situation is difficult. The oil industry employs only 8,000 persons (most of them are foreigners); only 2 percent of the arid land is under cultivation. Unemployment is high.

—the effects of the revolution on the Middle East arms race has been remarkable. The British had promised to provide one hundred Chieftain tanks to Libya, a not very maneuverable "anti-tank" tank. This was in line with the Treaty of Alliance and Defense between the U.K. and Libya, signed in 1953. Meanwhile, the French stole a march on the British with an agreement to sell 200 heavy tanks to Libya as well as 100 Mirage jets . . . or is it more than 100 planes? Reports have rumored sales of as many as 190 planes, including some which would not be Mirages. Regardless of the exact number, Libya hardly needs this much military equipment. The army numbers less than 10,000 men. It would seem that the planes and tanks could ultimately find their way to Egypt. To maintain the arms balance and in response to this huge sale, the United States has authorized new shipments of arms to Israel. The arms race increases . . . and seldom, if ever, has so much war matériel been accumulated without finally being used.

—the Idris government has promised an annual payment of $84,000,000 to the UAR. This was in line with the Khartoum conference which made it a matter of policy that oil-rich countries would pay for the military hardware of countries devoid of oil, releasing from this obligation only those oil-producing countries which had a revolutionary government. In other words, Algeria and Iraq were not required to furnish funds to the war chest of Egypt and Jordan, but Kuwait, Libya, and Saudi Arabia were under obligation. Under the new revolutionary and socialist regime Libya might well refuse to make further payments.

—Egypt has one important export commodity — teachers. They have now returned en masse to Libya from where they had been expelled at one point because of unceasing pro-Egyptian propaganda. The intellectual hegemony of Egypt is unquestionable. Through this corps of teachers the masses will increasingly accept Egyptian ideology. When Nasser was in Libya he received a tumultuous reception. Nasser is gradually unifying Libya, Sudan, and the UAR, embracing one-sixth of Africa, covering two million square miles. Nasser might envision a federation. The Soviets would benefit because cash-poor UAR and Sudan could pay in Libyan oil dollars for Soviet arms shipments. Such an arrangement would fall in line with Nasser's long range plan spelled out in his political testament.

—the new position of Libya may force Tunisia into a different political alignment. President Habib Bourguiba has often urged moderation and at times been branded as a traitor by other Arab nations. Tunisia had traditionally strong links with the West, including the United States and western Germany. In October 1966, Tunisia broke off all relations with the UAR, but they were resumed after the June war of 1967. Even then, Tunisia felt free to break off diplomatic relations with Syria in May of 1968. Encircled by strongly nationalistic countries, extremely belligerent toward Israel, and hostile to the West, Tunisia may not be able to maintain a realistic political position.

Regardless of possible changes in the Libyan government, be they to the left or to the right, toward conciliation or a more rigid Arab position, ultimately Libya will be in alliance with Egypt against Israel, according to Daniel 11. If present events are merely a dress rehearsal or the final line-up, makes little difference. In the end, Egypt, Libya, and the Sudan will play a significant role in the destiny of Israel.

SUDAN

Occasionally the Scriptures speak of the land of Cush. Sometimes the Hebrew word has simply been transliterated and so the KJV speaks of the land of Cush in Is. 11:11, where the RSV has Ethiopia. At other times the word Cush is translated Ethiopia in the KJV, as in Gen. 2:13, where the RSV reads Cush.

The exact geographic location or identification of Cush has been a matter of dispute. It is generally recognized that Gen. 2:13 refers to a Cush located in Asia. In most of the other places, Cush is found in association with Egypt. The Cushites lived south of Egypt, close to the Red Sea (and if they spread over to the other side of the Red Sea into the Arabian peninsula, it is easy to see why there might also be an Asian Cush).

In ancient times this area was called Ethiopia, but today the area occupied by ancient Cush is the equivalent of the modern Sudan. The name Cush appears in Egyptian sources, for the first time during the reign of Sesostris I (1971-1930 B.C.) to designate a relatively small area between the second and third cataracts. During the New Kingdom, the name took on a wider meaning, including most of the territory south of Egypt, an area usually known as Nubia. "The archaeologist Reisner excavated an Egyptian fortress dating from the 11th and 12th dynasties, with inscriptions from which it appears that this represented the colonial garrison of an indigenous Sudanese principality called Cush, lying between the third and fourth cataracts of the Nile."[8]

The kingdom of Cush emerged toward 1000 B.C. with Napata functioning as the capital. The kingdom came to an end toward A.D. 350. Previously the Cushites had enlarged their borders to the south, moving their capital to Meroe. The new frontier was probably a little to the south of Khartoum. "All this was the land of the blacks, and the Cushite dynasty henceforth ruled over a mixed population of Caucasians and Negroes, with the Negroes no doubt predominating."[9]

At times the country was very powerful and toward 750 B.C. the Cushites conquered large sections of Egyptian territory. At one point all of Egypt was under Nubian rule. One of the most famous kings was Tirhakah (690-664), mentioned in the Scripture in Is. 37:9 and 2 Kgs. 19:9 as an ally of Hezekiah in rebellion against the Assyrians. When Esarhaddon of Assyria invaded Egypt in 670 B.C., reducing it to a province of the Assyrian empire, the king of Nubia continued to rule at Napata. "The fly which is at the sources of the streams of Egypt" (Is. 7:18) was indeed the land of Cush, named by Isaiah along with Assyria as a first rate power. Invaded once again by Cambyses in 525 B.C., Cush appears in the list of Darius as a tribute-paying country (Esth. 1:1).

Ezekiel had announced that the land of Cush would fall into the hands of Nebuchadnezzar (30:1-10).

Most significant from the standpoint of prophecy is the fact that Cush is mentioned in Ezekiel 38 (v. 5) as part of the great invading force which will overwhelm Israel from the north. In Dan. 11:43 it is clearly stated that the antichrist shall gain control of Egypt and, quite naturally, those associated with Egypt, the Libyans and Cushites (unfortunately translated Ethiopians in both KJV and RSV), i.e., the Sudanese.

The final word of God regarding the Cushites is positive. They will stretch out their hands to God in adoration and ultimately recognize that the God of Scripture is the true God (Ps. 68:31; Is. 45:14; cf. Ps. 87:4; Zeph. 3:10).

At times the Scripture uses the word Cush to indicate remote nations to the south. This may well be the case in Is. 11:11. At the same time, there is no reason not to look forward to the actual fulfillment of the words concerning Cush or the Sudan, both in terms of cataclysmic conflict (Ezek. 38; Dan. 11) and ultimate conversion to God.

Traditionally the Sudan has maintained excellent relations with the United Kingdom. It is fair to say that in 1963 the Sudan played a neutral and moderating role in Arab League affairs. This was drastically changed after the June war of 1967. An army contingent was dispatched to the UAR and diplomatic relationships were severed with the United Kingdom and the United States. An arms deal was worked out with eastern European nations and 400 scholarships offered by eastern European countries were gratefully accepted. The fourth summit conference of Arab leaders was held in Khartoum and more recently, Egypt, Libya, and the Sudan have agreed to hold regular meetings every four months to coordinate their action against Israel in the military, political, and economic fields. After the abortive Arab summit conference in Rabat, the leaders of the three nations met in the Libyan capital in December of 1969 to coordinate the struggle with Israel.

Recently Sudanese strongman Major General Jaafar Nemery admitted that 1,000 Soviet military advisors and economic technicians had come to Sudan.

In the light of the prophetic statements these more recent developments are highly significant.

JORDAN

According to biblical sources the Ammonites were related to the people of Israel, which was the reason why the Israelites were not permitted to invade and conquer the country of the Ammonites (Gen. 19:38, Deut. 2:19). Originally the Ammonites occupied the area immediately to the east of the Jordan. The northern frontier was formed by the Jabbok River, and the northeast corner of the Dead Sea constituted the southern border. In the 13th century they were driven further east by the Amorites who occupied the fruitful Jordan valley. Compelled to move east, the Ammonites never gave up the claim to their ancient territory.

Israel took the land away from the Amorites and it became largely a possession of Reuben. About 300 years after the Israeli conquest the king of Ammon demanded peaceful restoration of the land. Jephthah pointed out that Israel

—had possessed the land for 300 years;
—conquered it from the *Amorites* and was therefore under no obligation to return it to the *Ammonites*.

In the light of contemporary events the claim of the Ammonites and the answer of Jephthah are significant. Today the roles are reversed but the answers still identical (Judg. 11:12 ff.).

The Ammonites were occasionally in conflict with Israel but defeated repeatedly. When the Solomonic kingdom split into Judah and Israel, the Ammonites took advantage of the resulting weakness to regain possession of the land east of the Jordan. We know very little about the Ammonites aside from biblical sources. Shalmaneser III mentions a contingent of one thousand Ammonites in the allied army which opposed him at Karkar in 853 B.C. About a century later Tiglath-Pileser III received tribute from Ammon. The Ammonites become vassals of greater powers, the superpowers of that day, first of the Assyrians and then of the Babylonians. The Ammonite kingdom lasted from about 1300 to 580 when Babylon gave it the coup de grace. Jeremiah predicted that they would be destroyed by Nebuchadnezzar (49:1-6). According to Josephus, this was fulfilled five years after the fall of Jerusalem (Jos. Ant. X:9:7).

As vassals of Nebuchadnezzar, Ammonite troops participated in the sack of Jerusalem. After the Jewish debacle the Ammonites took possession of some of the cities of Gad from which the Jewish population had been removed by the king of Babylon (Jer. 49:1-6).

Zephaniah predicted that an extreme calamity would fall on the land which would be like Gomorrah, desert and barren (Zeph. 2:9). Ezekiel announced that the territory would be desolate to the point where Rabbah, the capital, would be a place of pasture for camels. The prophet added that people of the east, i.e., nomadic tribes or Arabs would "make their dwellings in your midst" (Ezek. 25:4, 5).

It is possible that a few Ammonites returned to their country from the Babylonian exile, but by and large the area they had once occupied was now the home of the Nabateans. After the exile the Ammonites were leagued with the Arabs against the Jews (Neh. 4:7). They opposed the Maccabees and were soundly defeated (I Macc. 5:6, 7). There are fewer and fewer references to the Ammonites. Justin Martyr (c. A.D. 100-165) still mentions them as being rather numerous, but Origen (c. A.D. 185-254) includes the

country under the general name of Arabia. More and more
the area was infiltrated by Arabian Nabateans.

A word of Jeremiah deserves special attention. He de-
nounces the Ammonites but adds, "But afterward I will restore the fortunes of the Ammonites, says the Lord" (Jer.
49:6). It is not easy to determine what is intended by the
prophet: (a) Ammon will literally be restored. This was
fulfilled by a return from Babylonian captivity. But one
might object that Ezekiel had predicted that Arabs would
displace the Ammonites (Ezek. 25), a prophetic utterance
which was definitely fulfilled. The return of the Ammonites
was only "partial" . . . perhaps sufficient to justify Jeremiah's
words (?); (b) some expositors assume that the ultimate
conversion of Ammon is announced. They will be received
in the kingdom of God. It is difficult to point to a precise
fulfillment. The text does not favor this exegesis; (c) the
Ammonites will be restored in the latter days, even as Israel. This would then be fulfilled in the modern independent nation of Jordan. It is true that the Arabs are a
different ethnic group, but because they occupy the ancient
land of Ammon (Ezek. 25) all references to "Ammonites"
after the exile really concern the Arabs living in this region.
In fact, it could well be that this trend begins already in
Nehemiah. The Ammonites as such were never restored
but the word was used to designate the people living in the
land once occupied by the Ammonites.

In this connection one should also point to Isaiah who
predicts that the dispersed of Israel will be regathered from
the four corners of the earth and that all those who harass
Judah shall be cut off, including the Ammonites (Isa. 11:
11-14).

It may not be easy from the context to determine the
moment of this triumph nor its nature, but the distinct reference to the Ammonites might be significant. It is true that
they could be representative of ancient enemies in the immediate vicinity of Israel. But from a practical standpoint
this would make little difference.

Another reference to the Ammonites is found in Dan. 11: 41, indicating that "the main part of the Ammonites" shall escape the ravages of antichrist (because they are allies? . . . because of God's protective hand?)

Considering the different references just discussed it may be fair to speculate that ancient Ammon — an area occupied today by Jordan — will continue to play a significant role in the days to come.

After centuries of neglect and obscurity the land east of the Jordan River — for a while known as Transjordan — came back into the light of history. The country had to be practically rediscovered by 19th century explorers. The long Turkish control did little to improve the land. During World War I the Arab tribes, inspired by nationalism, rose up against the Turks. At the end of the war the area was directly administered by Great Britain. When the Amir Abdullah advanced against the French in Syria to avenge the defeat of his brother, he was dissuaded by the British with the promise to rule Transjordan. The League of Nations did give the mandate of Transjordan to the British who kept their word.

Relations between Abdullah and the British were cordial and at the beginning of World War II Transjordan was firmly on the side of the allies. After the war, on May 25, 1946, the relationship between Great Britain and Jordan was altered and the Hashemite kingdom of Jordan came into being under His Majesty King Abdullah I.

As a member of the Arab League, Jordan participated in troop operations against Israel which began with the termination of the British mandate over Palestine on May 15, 1948. When the Jordanian-Israeli armistice was signed, Jordan held about 2,000 square miles of central Palestine, including the Old City of Jerusalem. This area was incorporated into the Hashemite kingdom of Jordan on April 24, 1950, in spite of opposition from other Arab governments. In fact, only two countries recognized Jordan's annexation of the territory: Great Britain, because in a sense they had "fathered" the Hashemite kingdom of Jordan, and Pakistan, because the nation came into existence for religious reasons. The immediate Arab neighbors did not recognize Jordan's right over the West Bank. Since only two governments have formally recognized the annexation of the territory, Jordan's claim to the West Bank is weak from the international legal standpoint. Actually the inhabitants of these areas, often known as Palestinians, were not consulted. They are divided in their allegiance. Some hope for reunification with Jordan, others favor an independent Palestinian state.

The political climate changed after the assassination of King Abdullah in 1951. At first Jordan maintained closer relationships with Egypt and Syria, but later proclaimed a merger with Iraq. Relationships with neighboring Arab countries underwent changes as governments were toppled in Syria and elsewhere. The Jordanian cabinet was reshuffled from time to time. King Hussein escaped many attempted assassinations engineered by Arabs of differing political views both inside and outside of Jordan. The latest assassination attempt occurred on June 9, 1970, and was coincident with a week-long struggle between guerrilla forces and the Jordanian army. At one point the situation had deteriorated to the point where Syria offered arms to the Jordanians if they would overthrow King Hussein. In early 1967 Jordan had adopted an attitude of extreme hostility toward Arab revolutionary regimes, but as Jordanian-Israeli tension mounted, King Hussein signed a defense pact with the UAR (May 30). The June war of 1967 was disastrous for Jordan. The area west of the Jordan was lost. Casualties amounted to 6,094 killed and 762 wounded. The number of refugees increased. The economy suffered greatly and tourism diminished considerably (especially since the "Holy Places," i.e., Old Jerusalem, Hebron, Bethlehem, and others were in Jewish hands). Jordan could only survive thanks to massive doses of foreign aid from oil-rich Arab neighbors, the United States and other nations.

The current situation in Jordan is extremely complicated. No one suffered more from the 1967 war and gained less. King Hussein continues to rely on the United States (rather than the USSR) for arms shipments. In April of 1968, the United States State Department announced that an arms sales agreement had been reached with Jordan, possibly involving 100 M-48 Patton tanks and a dozen F-104 fighter jets. In July, the United States delivered some war matériel, especially tanks. Another thirty million dollar arms deal includes the sale of two squadrons of F-107 jet intercepters. In addition, the British have delivered a number of Centurion tanks as well as Hawk-hunter jets. Britain also agreed to sell Tigercat short range surface-to-air guided missiles.

King Hussein has conducted an almost worldwide personal and vigorous diplomatic campaign on behalf of Jordan. Assured of the loyalty of the Bedouin tribes, but not of anyone else, the king is hardly master in his own house. The Bedouins are outnumbered two to one by non-Bedouins in Jordan. It may not be easy to determine the total number of refugees but it could be as high as 500,000. How many have come in since 1967 is hard to know. For awhile they were able to return, but no more than 40,000 crossed the Jordan largely because of inefficiency on the part of the governments involved. Besides, some were afraid of Israeli occupation, others feared that their remittance checks sent by relatives from Kuwait or elsewhere would be cut off. For various reasons relatively few took advantage of the permission to return to the West Bank.

There are also approximately 20,000 fedayeen in Jordan, primarily loyal to Arafat. They almost constitute a state within a state. Perhaps as many as 17,000 Iraqi soldiers are still stationed in Jordan, not to mention Syrians and soldiers from Saudi Arabia. The Syrian soldiers arrived in Jordan without prior agreement. King Hussein's army may be 50,000 strong. Each group represents conflicting interests and the situation degenerates at times to the point of chaos.

Economically the presence of the fedayeen has been

beneficial. Jordanian dollar reserves are healthy. One of the most significant economic developments is related to the $85,000,000 East Ghor irrigation canal which supplies water to most of the eastern Jordan valley. The Ghor canal is part of an overall Arab plan to divert the sources of the Jordan River. The irrigation canal has occasionally been bombed by the Israeli airforce in retaliation for attacks originating in Jordan. It would almost seem as if there had been a gentlemen's agreement between Jordan and Israel not to attack certain sensitive areas. The Israeli port of Elat has not been attacked because retaliation would undoubtedly destroy the Jordanian port of Aqaba which would make Jordan dependent on Syrian ports for all supplies. Obviously the commandos have nothing to lose and will not be bound by such tacit agreements. On the contrary, they will do anything to increase the tension, hoping for the eruption of another war. The relationship between the king and the fedayeen has been extremely difficult and occasionally stress degenerates into strife.

In April 1969, King Hussein proposed a six-point program for a just and lasting peace in the Middle East, including free navigation in the Suez Canal and the Gulf of Aqaba. At the same time King Hussein pointed out that there could be no bargaining concerning the Arab sovereignty over Jerusalem. It is interesting that five fedayeen groups immediately issued a joint statement in Beirut repudiating the six-point program which had just been proposed. Israel dismissed the matter as a mere smoke screen since the king can hardly control commandos in his own country. This incident merely underscores and illuminates the extreme difficulty faced by the king both in relation to the Arab world and to Israel.

We have already considered the word of Jeremiah concerning the restoration of the fortunes of the Ammonites. Regardless of the exact interpretation which has already been discussed, it is self-evident that Jordan along with all the other countries of the Middle East will undergo a spiritual revolution upon the return of Christ. It seems that Jordan will be spared in the days of intense tribulation which will precede the return of Christ (Dan. 11:41). Regardless of the exact interpretation of these words, it is significant that again and again across the pages of the Old Testament God is seen as the God of all nations. Although he has chosen Israel for specific purposes, God never lost sight of the entire world. Even as he led Israel out of the land of Egypt so he brought "the Philistines from Kaphdor and the Syrians from Kir" (Amos 9:7). The heart and center of the *Old Testament* was the coming of the Redeemer and the proclamation of the forgiveness of sins. After the resurrection, Christ opened the minds of the disciples to understand the Scriptures, i.e., the Old Testament, and he said to them: Thus it is written that the Christ should suffer and on the third day rise from the dead, *and* that repentance and forgiveness of sins should be preached in his name to all nations, beginning from Jerusalem (Lk. 24:45-47).

LEBANON

For centuries the area now known as Lebanon was under Turkish control. The Turkish revolution of 1908 sparked an Arab nationalist movement, insisting on decentralization of the Turkish Empire and a measure of local autonomy for Syria — an area which at that time included Lebanon. During World War I the French occupied Beirut and the coastal area and hoped to become the mandatory power over a much larger region, including all of Syria. The population rejected the idea of a French mandate, but the San Remo conference of 1920 did give the French the mandatory power. The Syrians refused to recognize French authority but were defeated. The League of Nations approved the French mandate in 1922.

On September 1, 1920, the French established the state of Lebanon. For years France and Syria were involved in a protracted struggle which culminated in the independence of Syria. A separate treaty was established between Lebanon and France in 1936 in spite of Syrian opposition. According to the treaty, Lebanon was to become an independent state within three years, but the French failed to ratify the treaty.

At the beginning of World War II the French placed Lebanon under military rule. After the collapse of France the

Vichy government was recognized and in 1941 the British
and Free French reconquered Lebanon. In 1941 the French
officially announced the independence of Lebanon, but it was
only in August 1946 that the last British and French troops
left the country.

Approximately half of the Lebanese are Christians, mostly Maronites, Orthodox, Greek Melkites, and Armenian
(Gregorian). Lebanon enjoys religious freedom, including
the freedom of conversion! The country occupies a key
position in commerce and communication and is quite pros-
perous. Because of the ethnic and religious conglomerate,
Lebanon is in a precarious balance. The president of the republic is always a Maronite Catholic, the premier a Sunnite
Muslim and the speaker of Parliament a Shia Muslim. The
occasional political crisis is unavoidable. Beirut has become
a haven for exiled Arab leaders which has added to the con-
fusion and intrigue. Lebanon has close commercial links with
the other Arab nations which receive 50 percent of the Lebanese export consisting mostly of food, vegetables, and precious metals. On the other hand, links with western nations
are also strong in order to maintain a certain balance.

Tension with Syria is perpetual because

—the borderland is fertile and Syria would like control;

—the higher living standard in Lebanon has attracted
many Syrians. This influx of 250,000 Syrians up-
sets the Muslim-Christian balance and creates an effective fifth column for Syria.

—Syria would like to see militant action against Israel
in Lebanon.

For years Lebanon had managed to play a minimal role
in the Arab-Israeli conflict, barely participating in the 1967
war. This attitude is dictated by many different considerations. Economically Lebanese business would suffer. Tourism might decline if unrest pervaded the nation. The Lebanese army is small, numbering somewhere between ten and

fifteen thousand men, hardly enough to defend the frontier, let alone to attack Israel.

Lebanon was able to maintain this attitude until December 28, 1968, when the Beirut airport was attacked by Israeli helicopters and thirteen civil aircraft were destroyed. Militant elements in Lebanon demanded that the Palestine guerrilla organizations be given a free hand against Israel. A political crisis of the first magnitude developed, pitting Christians against Muslims and militants against conservatives (often equivalent to young against old). Arab guerrillas would like to use the Lebanese border against Israel because of the heavy vegetation in the area. This would be far superior to the bare Jordan Valley where guerrillas have suffered a casualty rate of 80 percent (dead) not to mention 2,000 prisoners. In the Jordan Valley every movement can be detected from helicopters. The Lebanese border would be an ideal "second front" for Al Fatah. The supply run from Syria to the southeast corner of Lebanon has already been dubbed the "Arafat trail" after Yasir Arafat, leader of Al Fatah. More is at stake. The guerrillas would like to control the refugee camps in Lebanon because the 160,000 Palestinian refugees are a prime recruiting ground. The guerrilla forces are backed by Syria and Iraq. In fact, Syria has sent terrorists into Lebanon under the guise of Palestinian commandos.

The Lebanese government has tried to curb guerrilla activities but without much success. The Lebanese regular army battled the guerrilla forces and casualties mounted on both sides. The country moved from crisis to crisis. Different compromise formulas failed. In August 1969 about 3,000 guerrillas representing five different organizations were concentrated in a small pocket of villages on Mount Hermon. This concentration made them vulnerable and Israeli air strikes inflicted heavy casualties. A bit later, in December of 1969, Lebanon promised to give full aid to the guerrilla forces but "within the framework of Lebanese sovereignty and security."

What is ultimately at stake is the control of the nation. None of the Arab governments is anxious to surrender the right to determine the scope of the conflict against Israel to a guerrilla organization. Lebanon is fearful of Israeli reprisal due to provocation by guerrilla forces and equally fearful of upsetting the precarious religious equilibrium.

The Israeli attack on the Beirut airport was unfortunate. It was in reprisal for an attack against an El Al plane for which an Arab guerrilla group with headquarters in Beirut took credit. Although the Lebanese government declined all responsibility, Israeli helicopters raided the Beirut international airport. The repercussions of the resulting crisis are still felt. Lebanon was almost compelled to take a more militant, anti-Israeli position.

It is true that guerrilla forces infiltrated Israel through the Lebanese border, but it would take an army of about 40,000 men to patrol the border effectively . . . and the Lebanese army consists of no more than 15,000 men. Under the circumstances fedayeen activity cannot be controlled by the Lebanese government. Christians who would like to maintain a more neutral posture are placed in an extremely difficult position. The role of Lebanon in "the next round" would probably have to be more militant than it has been so far . . . and the results could be disastrous for Lebanon.

From the standpoint of Scripture, it would appear that practically all of Lebanon is within the geographic confines of the promised land. The realization of the divine promise may not occur till the return of Christ. The previous occupation of the area by Israel might not at all be part of — in fact may even be contrary to — the divine plan.

Although the present population would strenuously resist any attempt by Israel to occupy Lebanon, the situation would be totally altered upon the return of Christ. Israel will turn to the Lord. The national life would be based on new, Christian principles. The spiritual would be the primary. The acceptance of Israel will be "life from the dead" (Rom. 11:15), i.e., Jerusalem will be a center of spiritual life for the entire world. This new relationship with God will alter all international contacts. Egypt and Iraq will also know God in a new, vital way (Isa. 19). The whole atmosphere in the Middle East will undergo a radical change and Lebanon will be glad to be part of the promised land. It will be an honor.

It is interesting that even now about one-half the population of Lebanon is non-Muslim. However, the radical changes of future events are both extraordinary and sudden (contrary to most historic developments which are slow and gradual) and therefore do not cast a shadow over the present situation. The future of Lebanon is one of glory and privilege.

IRAQ

Modern Iraq was carved out of the Ottoman (Turkish) empire by fusing the three Turkish provinces of Basra, Baghdad, and Mosul after World War I. These areas had been gradually occupied by Great Britain during the war. During the initial stages of this war Great Britain had promised the establishment of a national government, but at the same time the British government signed a secret Anglo-French agreement whereby Mosul would become a French sphere of influence. A nationalistic uprising occurred in 1920 but collapsed. The provisional Arab government which was established by the British was followed by the coronation of the Amir Faisal. At the same time the British mandate continued. After considerable treaty negotiation with Great Britain, Iraq was finally admitted to the League of Nations on October 3, 1932, thereby achieving statehood and the automatic termination of the mandate.

During World War II the temptation to flirt with the Axis powers was great, as anti-British feelings prevailed. Finally Iraq joined the fight against Germany.

In 1948 Iraq sent troops to Jordan to help in the fight against Israel. The short history of modern Iraq has been marked by an incredible number of coups. In February of 1958, a union between Iraq and Jordan was proclaimed, but the revolt and subsequent proclamation of the Iraqi republic (July, 1958) dashed these hopes. During 1964 Iraq moved very close to the UAR and there was much talk of union, but without concrete results. Iraq has often been at odds with its neighbors. It laid claim to oil-rich Kuwait and broke off diplomatic relations with countries recognizing Kuwait (including Jordan). This dispute was only settled in 1963. Iraq periodically feuds with Iran which is suspected of helping the rebellious Kurds. Approximately 20 percent of the population is constituted by Kurds who live in the mountainous crescent to the north and east. At times as many as 45,000 troops have been deployed against them. Except for the brief truce achieved in 1966, various Arab governments in Baghdad have tried to put down the revolution of the Muslim Kurds which was proclaimed on September 11, 1961, by their leader Mullah Mustafa Barzani. Some 15,000 Kurdish commandos have been fighting the Iraqi army. At stake is control of the rich oil fields of the Iraq Petroleum Company near Kirkuk which provides the necessary income enabling Iraq to fight both Israel and the Kurds.

In March of 1970, Lt. Gen. Ahmet Hassan Bakr, Iraq's president, granted the country's 1,500,000 Kurds most of what they wanted. The Kurds will finally govern their own territory and have the privilege to send delegates to the next Parliament. The Kurdish language will even enjoy official status along with Arabic. Of course, there have been previous arrangements which have not been kept but if the peaceful relationship persists it might spell more trouble for Israel since the Iraqi government will have a free hand to concentrate all military power against Israel.

There are many other minorities in Iraq, last but not least a Christian population of about 3 percent, mostly composed of Assyrians and Nestorians. Many live close to the Kurds who have guaranteed complete freedom of religion to all Christians. The Kurds proclaimed de facto autonomy in 1963. Relationships between the central government and the Kurds have alternated from all-out war to peaceful co-existence. More recently, villages with a majority of Christians have come under heavy aerial attack.

Internal problems (economic, minorities,) and external feuds (periodically with all Arab countries and of late especially with Syria), complicated by innumerable coups, have created an atmosphere of unrest and suspense which explains the recent sensational spy trials culminating in numerous hangings.

Iraq has pursued a violent anti-Israeli policy. During the war of 1967 thousands of troops were dispatched into Jordan. Two years later there were still 15,000 Iraqi troops in Jordan. Their purpose could be to:

—fight against Israel . . . but that activity has been minimal, limited to artillery shelling;
—uphold the government of King Hussein in Jordan, or
—help topple the government of King Hussein;
—make sure to safeguard Iraqi interests, over against Syrian interests;
—train Al Fatah commandos.

As far as the future is concerned, it has already been pointed out in the exegesis of Isaiah 19 that both Egypt and Assyria enter into a new relationship with God. Syria, or modern Iraq, will yet see a great spiritual revolution. The entire Middle East will become a center of spiritual life. The national conversion of Israel will inaugurate a new phase in world history. The immediate effect will be felt first of all in adjacent nations. Nationalism in its exaggerated form will yield to genuine co-existence because of a common center in the Prince of Peace. It is of course very difficult, and must to some extent remain a matter of speculation, to what extent the word of God is to be understood literally and how the word of God will be fulfilled — even if the prophecies are understood in their most literal sense. For example Jacob, speaking of Simeon and Levi, predicted that because of their violence they would be scattered in Israel (Gen. 49: 5-7). This was literally fulfilled. The tribes of Simeon and Levi were scattered across Israel. Simeon was absorbed by Judah. "Its inheritance was in the midst of the inheritance of the tribe of Judah" (Josh. 19:1 cf. Judg. 1:3). They did not occupy a specific territory like the other tribes.

Similarly Levi was scattered across Judah because the tribe was selected to function as priests and therefore they did not obtain a specific territory. The violence of their ancestor Levi was transformed into pure zeal for the Lord. The divine word was literally fulfilled but in the case of Simeon the tribe continued to play a minor role in the history of Israel, whereas in the case of Levi the tribe became a blessing to the entire nation. In other words, even when a literal fulfillment can be anticipated and actually occurs, it is still difficult to determine in advance how God will fulfill his word. Premature speculations should therefore be avoided or else be labeled as speculations in distinction from dogmatic assurance. Much of the prophetic concept must admittedly fall into the category of speculation, although individual Christians may have a very strong conviction regarding a prophetic program. It is a great temptation to become explicit where the word of God is silent and to forget that now we see in a mirror dimly and know only in part.

SYRIA

After centuries of Turkish rule Syria had hoped to become independent after World War I. A Syrian national congress elected a king in 1920 and a democratic constitution was drawn up for Syria, Palestine, and Transjordan. The allies, however, decided at the San Remo Conference in 1920 that Syria should become a French mandate. The French defeated the Arabs and took control of Syria. The mandate was approved by the League of Nations in 1922.

The struggle for independence continued and the French gradually yielded to pressure. In 1940, with the defeat of France, Syria came under the control of the Vichy government. The allies occupied Damascus in 1941. It was not till 1945 that Syria finally gained independence, but never achieved a stable government. A union with Egypt was short-lived. Instability and uncertainty became a way of life. If a year passes without a coup, an analysis is necessary to determine what went wrong. Tension with Lebanon (the border was closed for weeks in 1969), opposition to Nasser (especially in 1963), strained relations with Iraq, isolation in the Arab world, aggressiveness toward Israel, these were all vital elements of Syrian politics. Communist influence developed markedly in 1966.

Although the unqualified Syrian support of terrorist raids

was partly responsible for the Six-Day War, and in spite of an extremely belligerent attitude, the Syrians did not invade Israel, but used their artillery from high ground to shell Israeli positions. In the Six-Day War, Syria lost the least territory, suffered only minor casualties, and was saddled with the smallest refugee problem. The tough words were not backed up with action.

In 1969 the Syrian military chief of staff paid a visit to Peking. The Syrians were apparently unhappy with the slow USSR arms delivery. China was the first country to grant the Palestine Liberation Organization the status of a government in exile (a status not even granted by some Arab countries). A Chinese ship carrying arms arrived in Iraq and in spite of a Russian warning, Iraq granted Syria's request, permitting the ship to dock and unload. Mao's little red book is distributed in large quantities in Syria. At the same time, contacts with the USSR are maintained. The connection with China could be a piece of political blackmail or the first toehold of China in the Middle East.

The frontier with Israel was quiet for two years, but in July of 1969 the Syrian armed forces and air force launched an attack against Israel. Iraq has stationed approximately 6,000 troops in Syria but supporters of the Iraqi-backed Arab Liberation Front have been rounded up and arrested in Syria. The United Nations Security Council resolution of 1967 was never accepted by Syria which maintains an extremely belligerent stance in relation to Israel. In a recent vote, Syria won a seat in the United Nations Security Council for a two-year term, as one of the non-permanent members.

GUERRILLA MOVEMENTS

Even a cursory review of the recent history of the Middle East, the strenuous efforts of these nations toward independence, and the Anglo-French maneuvers, makes it evident why a negative attitude toward the West prevails. At one point U.S. prestige was high, especially whenever the United States opposed Great Britain and France and assisted Egypt. However, the good will of that era eroded rapidly when the Arabs felt — rightly or wrongly — that the United States was on the side of Israel.

On the other hand, political instability and economic stagnation of the Arab countries, the military defeat, and vacillation of internal and external politics all combined to frustrate the younger generation. It is not surprising that Palestinians especially, unwanted and devoid of official representation, have taken things into their own hands. The guerrilla fighters came into being and captivated the imagination of the masses, especially of young people and students.

The fedayeen are a relatively new development in the Middle East, but they have tremendous significance. Ever since 1967, commando raids into Israel have multiplied. The defeat of the Arab nations in the Six-Day War caused a tremendous disillusionment with the constituted governments. Guerrilla groups decided to take matters into their own hands.

In this case, as elsewhere, there is little Arab unity. There are a dozen major Arab commando groups. In 1967 the Palestine Liberation Organization (PLO) came into being to serve as a convenient channel for the distribution of funds received from regular Arab governments.

The best known guerrilla group is undoubtedly Al Fatah* under the magnetic leadership of Yassir Arafat. The beginning of Al Fatah is wrapped in obscurity, but in the mid-fifties, students formed political organizations, operating under the aegis of legitimate Arab governments. Often they came into sharp tension with established governments because they were used for subversive purposes by other Arab states. For instance, groups operating with the blessing of Syria might be most unwelcome in the UAR, etc. It was actually in Stuttgart, Germany, that Arab students formally established Al Fatah with the primary purpose of liberating Palestine. The aims were clearly outlined:

—since no reliance could be placed on established Arab governments, the Palestinians would have to initiate military action and fight for the liberation of Palestine;

—unable to conquer Israel, they swore to do everything in their power to provoke a military confrontation between the Arab states and Israel;

—they determined to inflict loss of life and damage on Israel;

—such commando action would destroy morale in Israel, and frighten potential immigrants as well as tourists. Ultimately the enemy would be provoked to violence which in turn would lead to more vio-

---

*The name is an acronym derived from the Arabic words Harakat al Tahrir al-Falastin, or Movement for the Liberation of Palestine. Its initials, H.T.F., form the Arabic word for death. They are ingeniously reversible to F.T.H., pronounced "faht," meaning conquest — hence Al Fatah or, as it is less commonly spelled, Al Fateh.

lence, escalating into war. Thus the primary purpose would be fulfilled, namely, to involve the Arab nations in the struggle against Israel.

Recruitment efforts were centered on students in Germany, Austria, Italy, Spain, and Yugoslavia. Some of the Stuttgart leaders made the customary pilgrimage of revolutionaries to Peking and were trained in guerrilla warfare. Algeria also served as an excellent training ground. Major training camps were established in Kuwait (heavily populated with Palestinians) and Algeria. Recruiting gradually focused on refugee camps.

Arms were received from Peking and became more plentiful after the Six-Day War. The battlefields were littered with arms abandoned by retreating Arab armies. For weeks, Al Fatah teams took camels into the Sinai Desert collecting machine guns, bazookas, and other weapons. Trucks and tons of ammunition were found and a large quantity of weapons obtained. The USSR had informed their client states that Soviet weapons should not be passed on to the fedayeen. Supplies came from other sources. By 1964 Al Fatah was ready for the first raid, sabotaging an Israeli water-pumping station. It is only since 1967 that Al Fatah is committed to launch an underground revolt among the Arabs who are now living on the West Bank. Hundreds of guerrillas crossed the Jordan River, but most of them were rounded up by Israeli forces.

Commandos are encouraged to strike day after day by the "voice of Al Fatah" and their exploits are reported night after night over radio Cairo. "Each night new Arab heroes are born, fresh revenge is meted out to Israel, a portion of Arab pride is restored." So much money is flowing to the fedayeen organizations that they are able to guarantee lifetime support for the families of all guerrillas killed in action.

It would appear that 20,000 fedayeen operate in Jordan and their ranks are swelling daily. Perhaps half of them are students, including many college students. Only since the 1964 Arab summit meeting have they received official Arab recognition.

In terms of political ideology the fedayeen ("those who sacrifice") are uncommitted, hoping that "the ideas will come out of the fighting." They generally envision a cleansing revolution in the conservative Arab nations and a Palestine in which Jews, Christians, and Muslims can live together in a "democratic, secular, socialist state."

The proliferation of guerrilla organizations has merged into four main streams:

—Al Fatah, by far the best known and the strongest, with its military arm Al Assifa (The Storm);
—Popular Liberation Army, an offshoot of the old regular Palestine Liberation Army;
—Al Asiqa (The Thunderbolt) largely at home in Syria;
—The Popular Front for the Liberation of Palestine (PFLP), by far the deadliest. This movement has been plagued with rifts and divisions and has given birth to the Popular Democratic Front for the Liberation of Palestine which in turn split into the Young Avengers and the Youth Which Will Return. The PFLP claimed credit for the attacks against the El Al airlines, the explosion at the Jerusalem supermarket, and other terrorist acts. Militant and marxist, their slogans are taken from Franz Fanon's *The Wretched of the Earth*: "Violence is a cleansing force. It frees the native from his inferiority complex and from his despair and inaction; it makes him fearless and restores his self-respect."

The fedayeen owe no loyalty to any government and are responsible only to themselves. In their eyes, any settlement with Israel is a betrayal and a disaster. In Jordan they virtually constitute a state within a state. They fight with the fanaticism and desperation of men who have nothing to lose. They have taken the destiny of the Palestinians into their own hands and carried the fight to Israel, thereby providing an outlet for the fierce Arab resentment. They have furnished a new sense of pride to a nation accustomed to defeat and humiliation. They have been idealized, especially in the person of their spokesman Yasser Arafat.

From the military standpoint they pose a serious problem. At one point, back in March 1968, Israel sent 15,000 troops across the border into Jordan to wipe out four Fatah bases. According to Jewish sources the action was so successful that the chief chaplain of the army stated that Israel "must have had divine sanction."

The question remains, of course, whether these different guerrilla groups really represent the vast majority of Palestinians. The fact that they have no clear agenda and that they are beyond the control of Arab governments makes them a dangerous and uncontrollable factor in the Middle East.

The Jordanian border hardly lends itself to infiltration. In addition, the Israelis have erected an electronic barrier stretching for about forty miles along the Jordan River valley. It consists of an outer line of eight-foot-high barbed wire and an inner, five-foot-high line ten yards away. The space between is laced with mines. At irregular intervals along the fence are strung electronic sensing devices which raise an alarm in adjacent guard posts when an infiltrator tries to cross. This is one reason why the fedayeen have been anxious to use Lebanon as a base and the Lebanese border as an infiltration area.

The psychological and emotional influence of the fedayeen is vastly superior to their number. Only in Jordan could they conceivably seize control of the government. However, this may be far removed from their real objectives. Since they are basically opposed to any form of settlement or peaceful co-existence the guerrilla movements will remain an extremely dangerous threat in the Middle East.

ARAB UNITY

It was a strange blessing when centuries ago the angel of the Lord announced to Hagar that her son would be "a wild ass of a man, his hand against every man and every man's hand against him; and he shall dwell over against all his kinsmen" (Genesis 16:12). The reference to the wild ass is most fitting. It is the image of the free, intractable bedouin character. The wild ass is untameable roaming at will in the desert, a wonderful symbol of the bedouin's boundless love of freedom.

The words "his hand against every man and every man's hand against him" are a fitting and vivid description of the incessant feuds among Arabs. To this day coups and counter-coups are the order of the day. "Without any connection to the Arab-Israeli conflict, the following took place:

1. Egypt at one time or another sent troops into Syria, Iraq, Kuwait, the Sudan, Algeria. Its armed forces have been engaged in hostilities in Yemen since 1962. Its air force has raided Saudi Arabian territory several times. It has attempted to instigate or support revolution in Syria, Lebanon, Iraq, Jordan, Saudi Arabia, and Yemen, not to speak of the western Arab world.

2. Syria has sent troops into Iraq and Jordan on some occasions and has attempted to instigate rebellion in both of them on other occasions.
3. Iraq has sent troops into Jordan, has massed troops to threaten Syria, and has attempted to instigate coups and rebellions there on more than one occasion.
4. Saudi Arabia has sent troops into Jordan a number of times, into Kuwait once, has supported with money and arms the royalists in Yemen against the Egyptians and the republicans since 1962, and has attempted to instigate rebellion and political assassination at one time or another in Syria, Jordan, and Egypt.
5. Jordan has sent troops into Kuwait, massed troops against Syria, and supported the Yemeni royalists at different times."[10]

Iraq and Syria still quarrel over the correct interpretation of Baathist socialism. A dozen guerrilla movements are competing with each other. It is only fear of Nasser's ambition in the Persian Gulf which brings Iran and Saudi Arabia together. Both supplied the royalists in the Yemen civil war against the Nasser-supported republicans.

The coup d'etat in Libya produced a major shift, since the fourteen member nations of the Arab League now contain a leftist majority for the first time. Eight states are counted among the more radical: Egypt, Iraq, Syria, Algeria, Sudan, the two Yemens, and Libya; over against this are six conservative governments: Morocco, Jordan, Saudi Arabia, Lebanon, Kuwait, and Tunisia.

A summit meeting was called in September 1969 with the avowed purpose of condemning Israel's annexation of Jerusalem. More than thirty-five nations were invited; twenty-four agreed to attend. It was the first summit conference ever held in fourteen centuries of Islamic history. The Islamic summit was sponsored by Egypt, Saudi Arabia, and

Morocco but Egypt quickly lost interest because of the predominantly moderate lineup. Nasser would not even attend the meeting, Syria and Iraq were boycotting the conference because only observer status was granted the Palestine Liberation Organization. The new revolutionary regime of Libya sent a low-level delegation and most of the black African Muslim countries — which receive substantial economic, technical, and military aid from Israel — remained absent.

The fifth summit conference also took place in Rabat but the formal opening of the session was delayed by procedural quibbles over the question of who should chair the meetings. A further delay was caused by disputes over the agenda. The immediate purpose of the summit conference was to promote Arab unity and to obtain additional funds for the UAR. It was almost unavoidable that the problem between Saudi Arabia and Yemen should poison the atmosphere. On the other hand, the Palestine Liberation Organization opposed all forms of settlement with Israel.

Ultimately no additional financial support was given to the UAR and unity was not achieved. Algeria favors a popular arms struggle against Israel whereas Saudi Arabia looks for long-range mobilization in order to win the war. The joint communique which was issued simply stated that Nasser and Feisal of Saudi Arabia had reached agreement on "the broad lines of Arab and Islamic strategy in the confrontation with Israel." They further added that they considered the Arab summit a "positive step towards the mobilization of Arab potentialities and further consolidation of the unity of the Arab struggle at this historic stage in the life of the Arab nation." In fact, Arab nations remain as fragmented as ever, devoid of inspiring and courageous leadership.

RUSSIA

Obviously Russia can hardly be considered a Middle Eastern power. However, it has played a dominant role in Middle East affairs in the last few years and cannot be ignored in any serious study of the area. At the same time, the attitude of the USSR has been of considerable interest to many Christians who feel that the mysterious references to Gog and Magog in the book of Ezekiel are related to a future role to be played by Russia.

The long standing historic interest of Russia in the Middle East has already been discussed. Until 1955 the Russian leaders had only demonstrated a peripheral interest in the Middle East. In that year, Egypt purchased military hardware from Czechoslovakia — hardly without an assenting nod from Russia. The USSR established diplomatic relations with Libya and a treaty of friendship with Yemen. The Russian mission in Damascus was raised to the level of an embassy. Almost overnight the Russians were entrenched in the Middle East, not by coercion or infiltration, but actually by invitation. As a matter of fact, the Communist party is illegal in all Arab countries — but not in Israel.*

---

*The Communist Party is operating illegally in Arab countries but membership is insignificant. Algeria: 900; Iraq: 2,000; Jordan: 700; Lebanon: 6,000; Morocco: 600; Sudan: 7,500; Syria: 3,000; Tunisia: 100; etc.

"Israel won a great battle in June 1967, but the fruits of that victory are being enjoyed not in Jerusalem but in Moscow. In the twenty months since the Six-Day War, the Soviet Union, trading on the desperation of the humiliated Arab states, has at last achieved objectives that had eluded its rulers ever since the eighteenth century. The most dramatic physical evidence of this lies in the fact that the Russians have finally realized their perennial ambition to become a major Mediterranean naval power. Far more ominous, however, the USSR has also become the major *political* power in the Middle East.[11]

The Soviet goal is a) to gain control of the Mediterranean basin and thereby to have the underbelly of Europe at their mercy; b) to control the Suez Canal and especially the Persian Gulf, which means control of Middle East oil, the lifeblood of western Europe; c) at the same time, new and additional pressure can be put on Turkey and Iran, threatening from both the south and the north.

The turning point of Russian influence came with the arms deal of 1955. A year later the U.S. commitment to finance part of the construction of the Aswan Dam on the Nile was cancelled and the challenge was accepted by Russia. In 1956 the number of students from the Middle East in the USSR increased enormously. Within a decade the USSR came to exercise a predominant position in the Middle East. Even NATO members like Turkey signed economic agreements with Russia. Turkey has reportedly begun to allow Soviet submarines to pass through the Bosporus at night, flouting the 1936 Montreux Convention. Iran signed a military agreement with the Soviet Union for $110,000,000.

It is well known that the USSR has shipped enormous amounts of military hardware to the Middle East and especially to Egypt. Only three days after Egypt responded to the Security Council's call for a ceasefire, on June 9, the Soviets agreed to rearm the Egyptian army. The role of the USSR is not easy. They would like to encourage permanent instability in the area but without allowing the situation to deteriorate to the point of open war against Israel. It is not easy for the USSR to control the Arab countries and practically impossible to restrain the Palestinian commandos who are under the leadership of Arafat. If the Arab governments are to some degree amenable to pressure from the USSR, the Palestinians are beholden to no one and dedicated to only one goal — the destruction of Israel.

If war were to break out

—the Arabs could be victorious, possibly compelling the United States to interfere, leading inevitably to a collision of the superpowers. Indeed, the USSR could hardly abandon their client states;

—Israel could be victorious and the USSR would be forced to help the Arabs, leading in turn to U.S. intervention.

This may be one reason why Russia maintains no less than 10,000 advisors in Egypt. At least 250 Russian pilots are flying MIGs with Egyptian markings, and at least twenty-five SA-3 missile sites have been installed in Egypt. The Russian presence could be a stabilizing factor, preventing Egypt from open warfare against Israel. On the other hand, the United Arab Republic can always threaten to turn to Peking for arms if the Russians fail to come to the rescue. It could be because of this potential Arab pressure that within six months after the June War of 1967, Russia replaced 80 percent of all the military equipment which had been lost by the Arabs. The arms shipments included 18 new Mig-21 fighters and SU-9 fighter-bombers, 200 tanks for Egypt, 40 planes and 100 tanks for Syria, and 20 planes for Iraq. Quite rapidly Egypt received about one billion dollars worth of Soviet military hardware. The larger military presence of the USSR in the Middle East may be an indication that their political influence has diminished. This military presence could be a political handicap since, instead of extending influence by proxy, the Soviets are now compelled to interfere more directly.

While the USSR has identified with the nationalist aspirations of Egypt, Syria, Iraq, Algeria, and Yemen, the United States has upheld the more conservative and traditionalist governments of Morocco, Saudi Arabia, and Jordan.

Under Russian leadership the Egyptian navy has become one of the most powerful in the world with no less than seven destroyers, twelve submarines, eighteen missile vessels, twelve antisubmarine boats and thirty torpedo boats.

Back in July of 1967 the Russian navy paid a courtesy visit to Port Said and Alexandria. The visitors consisted of one cruiser, one destroyer, two submarines, two guided missile carriers, five landing craft, and an oil tanker. From this modest beginning a large Russian fleet entered into the Mediterranean for the first time in history. Finally, a long-range Russian goal had been achieved.

The Russians use Egyptian bases to keep the United States 6th Fleet under perpetual surveillance. In addition they have some 6,000 to 15,000 troops and technicians in the Algerian naval base of Mers-el-Kebir. This is one of the best protected deep-water anchorages in the Mediterranean, complete with underground workshops and storage facilities which could even withstand a nuclear attack.

The Russians have even introduced a new multipurpose missile-firing helicopter carrier, the Moskva, into the Mediterranean. It can launch up to thirty helicopters of a type used in antisubmarine warfare. The Moskva is equipped with ship-to-air as well as ship-to-ship missiles.

Actually, the Russians use four Mediterranean ports: Algiers, Alexandria, Port Said, and Latakia in Syria. In addition, Russian warships have called at ports in the Sudan, Aden, Iraq, and Iran; and the Yemeni port of Hodeida is undoubtedly destined to become the base for Soviet operations in the Persian Gulf and the Indian Ocean. The Russian navy includes surface ships and submarines, some of which are capable of launching nuclear-tipped missiles. Generally, the Russians maintain thirty-five ships in the Mediterranean including nine submarines. The United States 6th

Fleet is normally composed of 50 ships, 25,000 men and 200 aircraft.

Submarine detection is particularly difficult in the Mediterranean because sonar tends to bounce off due to the difference in water temperature. Besides, the rock-strewn waters around Gibraltar provide an ideal cover for submarines.

The psychological and political effects of the Russian naval fleet in the Mediterranean make a significant impact in Europe and in the Middle East. The simple presence of a Soviet ship in a harbor may cause another nation to hesitate before retaliating for fear of Soviet military response. For instance, when the Soviet-made styx missiles, fired from an Egyptian torpedo boat, sank an Israeli destroyer in October of 1967, the Israelis did not retaliate for fear of hitting Soviet warships nearby.

The future of the Middle East may depend largely on the direction taken by Soviet policy. Interestingly enough, both Islam and Communism have lost ground in the area. Democracy seems like a far-out dream. The planned economy has not worked miracles, nationalism cannot serve as a guide to the perplexed. The breakdown of old beliefs and traditions and the absence of new values result in a deepening crisis, leading to creeping despair, seemingly cured only by radical solutions. This explains the frequent revolutions in the Middle East; the slow but continued drift toward anarchy persists. It could also become a golden opportunity for the proclamation of the gospel. The current spiritual vacuum might yet be used of God for the furtherance of His kingdom.

Gog and Magog

Jewish Views

The presence of the Russian navy in the Mediterranean and their tremendous influence in the Middle East is of particular interest to those who, on the basis of Ezekiel 38 and

39, feel that Russia has a significant role to play in the days to come. The mysterious words concerning Gog and Magog have always invited speculation. The ancient Rabbis, puzzled by the prophecies, were unable to reach a unanimous interpretation. Some placed Gog and Magog in the days of Messiah *son of Joseph,* who would either be victorious over Gog or, according to others, be killed. Some assumed that the wars of Gog and Magog were to take place before the days of Messiah, but others taught that the Messiah *son of David* would be victorious over Gog (Targum, Jerusalem on Num. 24:17; 1 Sam. 2:10). Again some Rabbis held the view that Gog and Magog would appear after the coming of Messiah but before the judgment. Rabbi Samuel commenting on Lev. 27:44 explained: "I will not spurn them" in the days of the Greek; "neither will I abhor them," in the days of Nebuchadnezzar; or "destroy them utterly" in the days of Haman; "break my covenant with them" in the days of the Romans; "for I am the Lord thy God" in the days of Gog and Magog (Megillah 11a).

The identification of Gog and Magog remained uncertain. Because the numerical value of the Hebrew letters of "Gog and Magog" equals seventy, it was easy to speculate that all seventy nations of the world (Gen. 10) would come against Jerusalem and there find their doom. Some fancied that Gog and Magog would come three times against Jerusalem even as Sennacherib and Nebuchadnezzar of old. Rabbi Akiba († c. 135) believed that the judgment against Gog and Magog would last twelve months (Eduyoth II:10).

Christian Viewpoints

Little solid information is gained from these rabbinical speculations. Christian interpreters have not fared much better. Different interpreters have placed the events

> —at the beginning of the millennium;
> —before the millennium, as part of the battle of Armageddon;

—after the millennium;
—both before (Ezek. 39) and after the millennium
(Ezek. 38).

Other exegetes have suggested that these chapters embrace all the deliverances to be experienced by Israel from the termination of the Babylonian captivity to the final gathering out of all the nations.

It could be that the imagery of Ezekiel's prophecy was based on the invasion of the Scythians. They lived north of the Black and Caspian seas on the Don and Volga rivers, spreading from there into Asia across the Ural mountains. In the seventh century they suddenly erupted into the civilized world of the Medes. They became known as a formidable power in western Asia, ruthless and cruel. They scalped their enemies and occasionally flayed them. They drank the blood of the first enemy killed in battle, and made drinking bowls of the skull of the slain, so that their ferocity and cruelty became proverbial (Herodotus 4:64, 65). They invaded Palestine and plundered the Temple of Venus in Ascalon (Ib. 1:105). Threatening to invade Egypt, they were bribed by King Psammetichus to desist. Only in 596 B.C. were they finally expelled from Asia. Ezekiel prophesied a few years later and, using vigorous, contemporary language, his descriptions were influenced by the recent events. The Scythians were so skillful in the use of the bow (Ib. 1:73) that Pliny thought them to be the inventors of bow and arrow (7:57). Famous to "shoot from horseback" (Herodotus 4:46) and renowned for "insolence and oppression" (Ib. 1:106), they were fit prototypes of earthly violence against the kingdom of God.

In the previous chapters (36 and 37), Ezekiel had announced the ultimate restoration of Israel, but the question might legitimately be raised: Will this regathering not lead to another dispersion? The power of the heathen world would still be overwhelming and finally Israel would find herself in exile once again. In answer to these doubts, the prophet gives the final reassurance that all of Israel's foes would perish. Even long after the ancient foes would have passed away from the stage of history (there is *no mention* of Ammon, Edom, Moab, Philistines, Syrians, Egyptians, Assyrians, or Babylonians in Ezekiel 38 and 39), new enemies from the extreme north will not be able to destroy the restored nation.

Who are the enemies denounced by Ezekiel? When shall these words be fulfilled?

Magog was identified by Josephus with the Scythians (Ant. 1:5:1), an elastic term covering the savage tribes living in the extreme north, i.e., north of the Caspian Sea. This general identification is confirmed by the immediate mention of *Meshech* and *Tubal*. The Moschi and Tibareni are mentioned by Herodotus as living in the mountains to the southeast of the Black Sea (3:94) in the 19th Satrapy of the Persians. Occasionally they spread as far as Cappadocia (Jos. Ant. I:6:1), but generally stayed in the mountains. Much earlier, in the records of Tiglath Pileser (1110 B.C.) the land of Musku is mentioned and located in the same area. Many of the Moschi crossed the mountains to the north, entering the vast steppes and mingling with the Scythians. They became known as Muskovs and the ancient Russian capital was named after them.

The association with Tubal is common in Akkadian sources. Shalmaneser II (860-825) mentions twenty-four princes of Tabal who paid tribute. Generally located around the Black Sea by different authors, they became typical of wild and savage nations (Ps. 120).

Herodotus describes the Moschi helmets made of wood and mentions their shields and spears of small size, with long spearheads (7:28).

Obviously Magog, Meshech, and Tubal are all three north of Israel, in an area occupied today by the USSR. G. R. Beasley Murray who expects the fulfillment of these chapters "after the commencement of the messianic kingdom" also states categorically regarding Meshech and Tubal that their "equation with Moscow and Tobolsk" is "unsupport-able" (*The New Bible Commentary,* in loco). Although strictly speaking, such an equation cannot be made, it re-mains true that these tribes lived in the mountains of Ar-menia and the Russian steppes (often spreading into the northeast of Asia Minor), an area largely occupied by the USSR.

There is one other problem. The ASV speaks of "Gog, of the land of Magog, *the prince of Rosh,* Meshech, and Tu-bal." This translation, accepted by many scholars, would strengthen the identification with Russia which was already made by the liberal exegete Hitzig back in 1847 and up-held by Gesenius.

The Persians (to the east) need no further definition. This area is occupied by modern Iran.

Cush has already been identified with the Sudan (to the south of Israel).*

Put is the area of Libya. "Insufficient evidence pre-cludes certainty, but few objections could be raised against the equation of Put and Libya" (I.D.B., art. Put)**.

Gomer is usually identified with the Cimmeranians who lived north of the Black Sea and gave their name to the Cri-mea. Expelled from their ancient habitation by the Scythi-ans, they moved into Asia Minor and upon their defeat (c. 580 B.C.) on to northern Europe.

Bethtogarmah has always been identified with Armenia.

All in all, a powerful confederacy is described under the leadership of northern nations (largely located in mod-ern Russia), but including eastern and southern enemies as far away as Libya.

This invasion will take place "after many days," "in the latter years" (vv. 8, 16) — rather indefinite indications. Ezekiel 38:8 is more definite. The assault will be "against

---

*References to an Arabian Kus to the north or a nation called Kasse (between Edam and Media) are less probable.
**The identification with Punt, connected with the coast of Somali-land, is less probable.

the land that is restored from war, the land where people were gathered from many nations upon the mountains of Israel, which had been a continual waste; its people were brought out from the nations and now dwell securely, all of them." These events will occur following a prolonged exile and restoration of Israel. This would certainly favor a period before or at the beginning of the millennium. The result of the divine intervention will be that "all the nations will see my judgment" (39:21), Israel will really come to God (39: 22 ff.), and God will pour out his Spirit upon the house of Israel (v. 29). The manifestation of God's glory among the nations could point to a fulfillment after the millennium which is supported by Rev. 20:7 ff. If Gog and Magog are used symbolically in Revelation 20 (simply representing enemies of God's kingdom), a figurative exegesis may also be applied to Ezekiel 38 and 39, treating it as a prophetic parable. A totally literal interpretation of these two chapters should not be attempted. For instance, the weapons mentioned by Ezekiel are hardly relevant or significant for our day.

The symbolic view is strengthened by 38:17: "Are you he of whom I spoke in former days by my servants the prophets of Israel, who in those days prophesied for years that I would bring you against them?" Since there is no reference to Gog anywhere else in the Old Testament it has been argued that only the basic aim of many other ancient prophecies — namely the proclamation of the ultimate triumph of God's kingdom — is echoed by Ezekiel, and it is therefore pointless to look for a more detailed fulfillment.

We are obviously faced with many exegetic difficulties which have given birth to different interpretations. It would be unwise to be dogmatic. Some things are relatively clear: After a long period of exile, Israel will be restored. The setting is totally different from previous historic experiences (the ancient enemies are no longer mentioned). Israel will face an invasion led by armies from the north, but in league with other powers to the east and south. The nations mentioned in the prophecy are living at the edge of the civilized world as it was then known. The ancient home of these ancient tribes is occupied today by the USSR — which is at any rate today's great northern power in relation to Israel. The speculation is tempting that a Russian invasion is predicted. Allied with nations as far south as Libya and Arab nations to the east, the invaders will cover the land like a cloud, only to be defeated by the power of God. Russian involvement in Middle Eastern affairs, their close alliance with Arab nations (although previously an ally of Israel in order to dislodge the British from the Middle East), their new presence in the Mediterranean, the strategic significance of Israel, Middle East oil — these and other factors make such an interpretation quite possible. Dogmatism would be totally out of place. Political alliances can change and former enemies become allies. But the particular viewpoint just mentioned (held by many Christians) would seem to be justified by the words of Ezekiel. Admittedly, this interpretation is to some extent conditioned by the contemporary situation and must therefore remain speculative. It remains true, however, that at some future point Israel will suffer an invasion from the north by an enemy who has allies both to the east and south of Israel.

The USSR holds an important trump card — over two million Jews live in Russia. Only a few hundred older Jews leave Russia each month for Israel. The Israeli government is extremely anxious to welcome these Russian Jews. For one thing, they are under pressure in the USSR, and most of all, Israel desperately needs immigrants to maintain a certain population balance. Aside from the United States (and Jews in the United States show no signs of leaving for Israel en masse) the USSR is the last great reservoir of potential Jewish immigration. This situation gives the Russian government a great deal of leverage. In return for two million exit permits, Israel might well settle the boundary dispute in favor of the Arabs. The Arab nations would be upset over the influx of two million Jews into Israel but they could be persuaded to accept this situation given enough concessions in other areas. Since the USSR has tremendous influence over its client states (Egypt, etc.) and great bargaining powers with Israel thanks to two million potential hostages, she is in an ideal position to dictate the terms of a Middle Eastern peace. The USSR prefers by far to maintain an unstable situation, to keep the Suez Canal closed (hurting the economy of western Europe and Egypt), to maintain the Arab states in a position of dependency, to keep the Jews in Russia as potential hostages, gaining maximum advantage through minimum efforts. In fact, if Russia were to use her influence to settle the Middle East problem, she would immediately lose her usefulness to the Arab nations which would only result in a political disadvantage to the USSR. In the last decade Russian political and economic gains in the Middle East have been tremendous and one can expect a high degree of continued Russian involvement in the area — ultimately leading up to the situation described by Ezekiel.

Note:

The identification of Gog has also been debated, but certainty cannot be achieved. According to the *New Bible Commentary,* Gog could be derived from *Gagaia,* home of barbarians mentioned in Amarna letters. According to *Eerdman's Bible Dictionary,* "the only reasonable identification of Gog is with Gyges, King of Lydia (c. 660 B.C.) . . . Assyrian Gugu." There are many other views. Gog has been connected with Gagaya which is sometimes used as a synonym for barbarian. Others have connected it with the Assyrian gagu describing a land to the north. The identification with Gyges, king of Lydia, is considered "less probable" by F. Brown (in the article Gog and Magog in the E.B.) The identification must remain uncertain.

THE ISSUES

It has been suggested by some analysts that the real issue is between Arab pride and Jewish survival, but this analysis is too superficial. As I. F. Stone put it: "Stripped of propaganda and sentiment, the Palestine problem is, simply, the struggle of two different peoples for the same strip of land. For the Jews, the establishment of Israel was a Return, with all the mystical significance the capital R implies. For the Arabs it was another invasion. This has led to three wars between them in twenty years. Each has been a victory for the Jews. With each victory the size of Israel has grown. So has the number of the Arab homeless.

"Now to find a solution which will satisfy both peoples is like trying to square a circle. In the language of mathematics, the aspiration of the Jews and the Arabs are incommensurable."[12]

Walter Laqueur concluded an article entitled "Is Peace in the Middle East Possible?" with the doleful words: "There is no cure for the Middle East sickness, but there is one sure way to alleviate it: to reduce the problems to their real size . . . half the battle for the future of the Middle East will be won on the day when news about this part of the world will be relegated from Page 1 to Page 16 in *The New York Times* and other leading newspapers."[13]

It is questionable whether time will really be the healing

factor since in the last twenty years this conflict has erupted three times. The author has very nicely summed up the contrast between the Arab and the Jewish viewpoint. As to the former "their case is well known; Palestine was an Arab country up to the end of World War I, when Britain imposed the Jewish community on the Arabs, who were thus asked to atone for the sins of the Christian peoples of Europe. Following Zionist invasion and aggression, the Jewish refugee problem was solved by creating an Arab refugee problem. The establishment of a Jewish state was thus a crying injustice; moved by collective guilt feelings about the Jews, the European peoples ignored the fact that morally, and in every other respect, right was on the side of the Arabs.

"The case is familiar, and so are the counterarguments: that Palestine was a Turkish province inhabited by a few hundred thousand Arabs at the time of the Balfour Declaration; that Jerusalem had a Jewish minority well before 1917; that Zionism has built up a flourishing country from what was largely desert; that a Jewish state came into being because the Arabs rejected a binational state; that Israel expanded beyond the borders of the United Nations resolution of 1947 as a result of invasion by Arab armies; that the loss of a war is a misfortune, but not a moral argument; that nations have never come into being in accordance with the moral law, but as the result of migration, settlement, invasion and other forms of peaceful, or not so peaceful, conquest. All this is familiar; no useful purpose will be served by pursuing this discussion."[14]

The Middle East problem is further complicated by the great religious significance of Jerusalem, the enormous refugee problem, and fear — fear on the Arab side of Israeli expansion and fear on the Israeli side of the overwhelming numerical superiority of the Arab world.

In order to gain an adequate perspective on the contemporary situation it is necessary to retrace the background at least to some extent, especially as it relates to the Jewish people and the land of promise.

THE JEW AND THE LAND

Jerusalem has always exercised an extraordinary fascination on Christians, Jews, and Muslims alike. Christian concern is ancient indeed. Soon after the fiasco of the crusades, the Franciscans tried to establish a foothold in Jerusalem (1219). They managed to obtain control of a church in 1333 which was lost about 200 years later, but managed to reestablish themselves in 1559.

Because of the significant number of Jews in Jerusalem, a Boston Mission Society sent out two missionaries in 1818 followed by a British effort in 1832. To protect the British missionaries a consulate was established in Jerusalem in 1839. Toward that time the Turkish empire seemed near dissolution. Mohammed Ali Pasha of Egypt almost controlled Turkey. The European powers intervened in the Turko-Egyptian conflict and Egypt was compelled to abandon all claims to the Holy Cities. The weakened condition of the Ottoman empire seemed to create an ideal opportunity to establish a Protestant Bishopric in Jerusalem and King Frederick William IV of Prussia decided to act in conjunction with the Archbishop of Canterbury. The bishop of Jerusalem was to be appointed alternately by the crown of England and Prussia. The first bishop was a converted Jew, Michael Solomon Alexander, professor of Hebrew and

Rabbinic literature at Kings College. He entered Jerusalem on January 21, 1842. He died shortly afterwards (1845) and was followed by the well-known Samuel Gobat. In 1845 the Greek Orthodox Patriarch moved his seat from Constantinople to Jerusalem and Rome renewed the Latin Patriarchate in 1847.

Toward the turn of the century the population of Jerusalem was about 60,000, of which 41,000 were Jews (mostly poor), 12,800 Christians of various denominations, and 7,000 Muslims. The turn of the century witnessed two significant developments: Zionism and the birth of Arab nationalism.

It is true that Jews have remained attached to the land of promise across the centuries and regardless of dispersion. Jewish prayerbooks frequently echo the desire to return to the land. At times the vision was dim and "the interest in a return of the Jews to Palestine was kept alive in the first part of the 19th century more by Christian millennarians especially in Great Britian, than by Jews themselves (*Encyl. Brit.*, "Zionism"). Mention has just been made of the establishment of a Protestant Bishopric in Jerusalem. Here and there lone Jewish voices pleaded for return to Zion coupled with a moral and spiritual regeneration. A few Russian Jews settled in Palestine. Some only hoped for a Jewish cultural center in Palestine, radiating spiritual influence.

Theodore Herzl was almost driven to Zion because of the prevailing anti-Semitism, especially crystallized in the Dreyfus affair in France. Herzl would have preferred assimilation but felt that it was utopian. "Herzl had no living ties with Jewish and Hebrew traditional values. He never desired the rebirth of Hebrew as a national language" (ib.). Zionism was a political movement. The first Zionist Congress was convened in 1897 in Basel, Switzerland, and the objective of Zionism was clearly defined: To create for Jewish people a home in Palestine secured by public law.

The center of Zionism was Vienna, home of Theodore Herzl. The chaplain to the British Embassy in Vienna was

Rev. William H. Hechler, keenly interested in the restoration of the Jews in Palestine. He helped arrange meetings between Herzl and leading personalities including the Grand Duke of Baden and was present at the first Zionist Congress. Although Zionism represented only a minority of Jews it became a powerful force because of its worldwide organization and especially due to the renewed persecutions of 1905 in Russia. By 1914 there were 90,000 Jews in Palestine, including forty-three agricultural settlements.

The ferment of nationalism reached the Arab world in 1905 when N. Azouri, a Christian Arab, demanded the autonomy of Arab lands from the Turkish empire. The movement gathered momentum and during World War I pinned all hopes on Great Britain, aspiring to the creation of a single Arab state. The first Arab Congress was held in Paris in 1913 and was attended mostly by delegates from Syria and Lebanon. Of the twenty-four delegates, eleven were from Christian communities. But the movement failed to gather momentum partly because of Anglo-French rivalry and also because the Arab masses were unwilling to be separated from the Sultan of Turkey who was the head of all Islam and Master of the Holy Muslim cities of Mecca and Medina.

The idealistic proclamation of pan-Islamism (especially by Abdul Hamid II, 1876-1909) remained fruitless and was followed by a new emphasis on nationalism. Given the diversity of Muslim countries, nationalism inevitably produced disintegration of Muslim unity. Nationalism triumphed when most Arab nations finally did gain a measure of autonomy from the Ottoman empire after World War I, affecting Lebanon, Jordan, Libya, Sudan, Tunisia, and Morocco. At the same time the drive for greater Arab unity continued and resulted in the creation of the League of Arab States (March 1945).

That political Zionism and Arab nationalism would clash head-on was easy to foresee. The British played a significant role in subsequent developments. First Sir Henry

McMahon (1862-1949), British High Commissioner in Cairo, negotiated with Sharif Hussein of Mecca. He had approached the High Commissioner in July 1915, offering Arab aid against Turkey if Britain, in return, would pledge support of Arab independence within a territory clearly specified by Hussein. The British promised to recognize and support the independence of the Arabs within the limits demanded by the Sharif of Mecca. The British government later contended that Palestine was *not* included in the British pledge of Arab independence. If the McMahon promise had been respected, Amir Feisal would have been the head of an extensive Arab state with its capital in Damascus, and Abdulah would have been made king of Iraq. The British have always denied that the McMahon letter included Palestine which was not mentioned by name in this correspondence. The statement was ambiguous and read: "the districts of Mersina and Alexandretta and portions of Syria lying to the west of the districts of Damascus, Homs, Hama, and Aleppo cannot be said to be purely Arab, and should be excluded from the limits demanded."

At any rate, when Feisal claimed his throne and entered Damascus in 1920 the French were there before him in accordance with another treaty signed with Great Britain. The Sykes-Picot treaty was a secret agreement between the British, the French, and the Russians to divide the Asiatic provinces of the Ottoman empire. An independent Arab state was envisioned but only for the area now known as Saudi Arabia and Yemen. France was to occupy Lebanon and Syria, Britain would control Iraq and Transjordan, and parts of Palestine were to be placed under international administration.

At the same time, the British continued to encourage Jewish ambitions and on November 2, 1917, Arthur James Lord Balfour sent a letter to Lord Rothschild which became known as the Balfour Declaration: "His Majesty's Government views with favor the establishment in Palestine of a national home for the Jewish people, and will use their best endeavors to facilitate the achievement of this object, it being clearly understood that nothing shall be done which may prejudice the civil and religious rights of existing non-Jewish communities in Palestine, or the rights and political status enjoyed by Jews in any other country."

Carefully worded, the Declaration promised only "a" (not "the") Jewish national home "in" Palestine (not a Jewish state). The British government did not intend to create a Jewish state in Palestine. The declaration generated a great deal of enthusiasm among the Jews, although it fell short of Zionist goals. Arab reaction was predictable. Although Arab nationalism was primarily anti-Turkish, it was also anti-Zionist. A wave of anti-Jewish activity began in Galilee late in 1919 and violent Arab riots took place in Jerusalem in 1920.

It is true that Amir Feisal, who in 1921 became king of Iraq, signed an agreement with Dr. Chaim Weizmann but he added the reservation that his letter would be binding only if the British carried out the project of an Arab state. In correspondence with Mr. Frankfurter, Feisal declared: "We feel that the Arabs and Jews are cousins in race, having suffered similar oppressions at the hand of powers stronger than themselves, and by a happy coincidence have been able to take the first step toward the attainment of their national ideals together.

"We Arabs, especially the educated among us, look with deepest sympathy on the Zionist movement . . . we will do our best, as far as we are concerned, to help them through, we will wish the Jews a most hearty welcome home . . . our two movements complete one another. The Jewish movement is national and not imperialistic, and there is room in Syria for us both. Indeed, I think that neither can be a real success without the other." It must be remembered that in this context Syria included Palestine.

President Woodrow Wilson dispatched an all-American King-Crane commission to determine which of the western nations should act as the mandatory power for Palestine.

The commission toured the area in June and July 1919, and recommended "that the unity of Syria be preserved . . . the country is very largely Arab in language, culture, traditions and customs." They suggested that Lebanon be given a large measure of local autonomy and that Amir Feisal be made the head of the new united Syrian state. As to Palestine, they pointed out that "the extreme Zionist Program must be greatly modified. For 'a national home for the Jewish people' is not equivalent to making Palestine into a Jewish state; nor can the erection of such a Jewish state be accomplished without the gravest tresspass upon the 'civil and religious rights of existing non-Jewish communities in Palestine.' The fact came out repeatedly in the Commission's Conference with Jewish representatives, that the Zionists look for a practically complete dispossession of the present non-Jewish inhabitants of Palestine, by various forms of purchase."

The Commission then pointed out that the non-Jewish population of Palestine was nearly nine-tenths of the whole and that they were emphatically opposed to the Zionist Program. They further opined that "the initial claim, often submitted by Zionist representatives, that they have a 'right' to Palestine, based on an occupation of 2,000 years ago, can hardly be seriously considered." They added that "with the best possible intentions, it may be doubted whether the Jews could possibly seem to either Christians or Muslims proper guardians of the Holy places, or custodians of the Holy Land as a whole."

Nevertheless, the Balfour Declaration was publicly endorsed by the various allied and associated powers and the San Remo Conference held in April 1920 decided that the mandate for the government of Palestine should be entrusted to Great Britain. This was confirmed by the League of Nations.

Gradually Jewish immigration increased and Arab opposition hardened. An economic crisis reversed the trend temporarily so that in 1927 emigration of Jews from Palestine exceeded immigration. By 1929 serious Arab riots broke out and it took two years to restore order in Palestine. An Arab revolution of unprecedented scope began in 1936 and a Royal Commission was sent to Palestine to investigate the problem. In 1937 the Peel Commission reported that partition was the only solution because "an irrepressible conflict has arisen between two national communities within the narrow bounds of one small country. About one million Arabs are in strife, open or latent, with some 400,000 Jews. There is no common ground between them." They suggested that the mandate be terminated and that Palestine be partitioned. The Jewish state was to comprise about 20 percent of the area of the country, and the rest, Arab Palestine, was to be united with Transjordan. Jerusalem, Bethlehem, and a small area would remain a British mandatory zone. This plan was immediately rejected by Arab leadership and accepted by the Zionist Congress with qualifications. The British government rejected the findings of the Peel Commission. The Arab revolt was quelled by the British and a new commission dispatched. The Woodhead Commission saw enormous obstacles in any plan involving partition. The British then published the famous White Paper in May of 1939 which

—declared that the establishment of a Jewish state in Palestine was contrary to British obligations to the Arabs;
—promised the establishment of an independent Palestine after a period of ten years;
—limited Jewish immigration to 75,000 over the next five years. After the five years, no further Jewish immigration would be allowed except with Arab consent. Jewish reaction was bitterly hostile and Arab leaders also rejected the White Paper.

World War II interrupted the crisis which resumed almost immediately at the end of hostilities, in 1945. After

the war, Great Britain invited the United States to partici-
pate in finding a solution to the problem and an Anglo-
American inquiry committee was appointed in November
1945 to examine the status of the Jews in the countries
which had been occupied by Germany, to determine how
many would be compelled by their condition to migrate.
Their recommendation included the statement that "Palestine is not, and never can be a purely Jewish land. It lies
at the crossroads of the Arab world. Its Arab population,
descended from long time inhabitants of the area rightly look
upon Palestine as their homeland." They also recommended
the admission of 100,000 immigrants, victims of Nazi perse-
cution, as soon as possible.

Immediately after the war, Jewish terrorism against the
British became a fact of life in Palestine (1944-1946). The
impossibility of achieving a compromise solution between
Jews and Arabs led the British to refer the Palestinian problem to the United Nations in February of 1947. At one
point a United Nations special committee suggested a seven-
fold partition. Fortunately this fantastic proposal was defeated by the General Assembly. In Palestine, a guerrilla
struggle raged. Many Arabs, especially from the upper
class, fled the country. The massacre by Jewish terrorists of
250 Arab women and children at Dair Yasin (April 19,
1948) created near panic conditions. Debate in the United
Nations continued. Finally, on August 31, 1947, the United
Nations published the recommendations of a special committee on Palestine. Partition was recommended and a partition plan was accepted by the Jewish Agency as the "indis-
pensable minimum." The Arab governments and the Arab
higher executive rejected it. On November 29, 1947, the
United Nations General Assembly endorsed the partition
plan. It is entirely possible that the partition plan was favored over against a federation concept only because a
greater degree of cooperation was necessary for the latter.
The partition plan did contain the concept of economic col-
laboration and economic union. Jerusalem was to be placed

under an international trusteeship system (ITS) which would designate the United Nations as the administering authority. It is worthy of note that the Russians strongly backed the partition plan, and favored the creation of a Jewish state. Their primary purpose was to expel the British from the Middle East. Israel received a significant shipment of Russian arms which was of crucial significance in the war of 1948. Actually, opposition to the partition plan was largely spearheaded by the United States and Great Britain; in fact, Britain refused to vote in favor of the partition plan. John Foster Dulles argued that the United Nations had no legal right to deal with the Palestinian problem. His motion was defeated — largely through Russian influence — by twenty-one to twenty. Russia was the first government in the world to give the new State of Israel full official recognition.

At the time of the partition less than 6 percent of the total land area was owned by Jews. Arab land ownership was slightly below 50 percent. The balance of the land was "public land." The partition plan gave 57 percent of the total land area to the Jewish State and 43 percent to the Arab State. The plan also envisioned a significant Arab minority of no less than 40 percent within the Jewish State.

The United Nations partition plan envisioned that the mandate for Palestine should terminate as soon as possible but, at any rate, not later than August 1, 1948. On May 14, 1948, a Proclamation of Independence was published by the Provisional State Council in Tel Aviv. The opening statement reads: "In the land of Israel, the Jewish people came into being. In this land was shaped their spiritual, religious, and national character. Here they lived in sovereign independence. Here they created a culture of national and universal import, and gave to the world the eternal Book of Books."

The declaration makes mention of "the right of the Jewish people to national restoration in their land," and speaks of "the historical connection between the Jewish

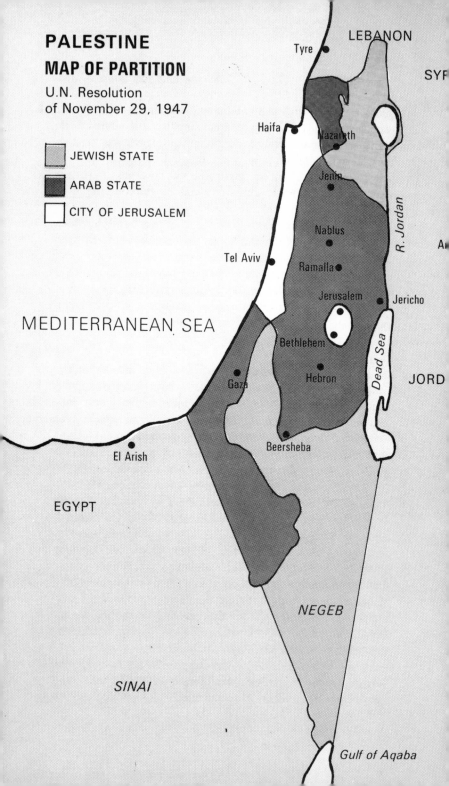

people and the land of Israel." Aside from a fleeting reference to justice and peace as envisioned by the prophets of Israel and a concluding statement expressing trust in the rock of Israel, there is no reference to age-old prophecies concerning the return to the land nor acknowledgement of God's sovereignty or leading. The right to the land is somewhat taken for granted. It is simply stated that Theodore Herzl "gave public voice to the right of the Jewish people to the national restoration and their land." This "right" was acknowledged in the Balfour Declaration, confirmed by the mandate of the League of Nations and referred to in the United Nations resolution calling for the establishment of a Jewish state in the land of Israel. "It is a natural right of the Jewish people, like any other people, to control their own destiny in their sovereign state."

The War of Independence, as it is called by Israel, was marked by extremely heavy losses, namely 1 percent of the total Jewish population. In fact, 4,487 servicemen and women fell in the War of Liberation. The war of 1948 came to an end, and armistice agreements were signed with Egypt, Lebanon, Jordan, and Syria. As a result of the fighting Israel seized 23 percent more territory than had been allotted to her by the 1947 partition plan. As much as 80 percent of the total Palestinian territory came into Jewish hands.

Israel was admitted to United Nations membership on May 11, 1949. On December 9, the United Nations General Assembly decided that Jerusalem should be placed under a permanent international regime with appropriate guarantees for the protection of the Holy Places both within and outside Jerusalem. The area would be administered by the United Nations. The city of Jerusalem would include not only the present municipality and surrounding villages, but also Bethlehem.

Another United Nations resolution dated September 1, 1951, referred to Egyptian interference with passage through the Suez Canal of goods destined for Israel. The United Nations called upon Egypt to terminate all restrictions on the passage of international commercial shipping and goods through the Suez Canal.

Unrest and tension increased in the area. From the end of the War of Liberation till the Sinai Campaign at the end of 1956, Israel lost 1,176 servicemen.

In 1956 Israel, Britain, and France invaded Egypt in the famous "100-Hour War." The Israeli objective was to destroy the Egyptian raiding bases, to open sea communications through the Gulf of Aqaba, and to pressure Egypt into serious peace negotiations. Britain and France sought control of the Suez Canal, which Egypt had taken over, but U.N. (and U.S.) pressure forced an end to the hostilities. The Sinai Campaign claimed 191 Israeli lives. The uneasy peace which followed lasted until 1967. During that time another 893 Israelis died in the line of duty.

The outbreak of the Six-Day War should not have surprised anyone. In Nasser's speech to Arab trade unionists of May 26, 1967, he said: "Taking Sharm el-Sheik meant confrontation with Israel. Taking such action also meant that we were ready to enter a general war with Israel. It was not a separate operation . . . We sent reconnaissance aircraft over Israel. Not a single brigade was stationed opposite us on the Israeli side of the border. All Israeli brigades were confronting Syria . . . If Israel embarks on an aggression against Syria or Egypt, the battle against Israel will be a general one and not confined to one spot on the Syrian or Egyptian borders. The battle will be a general one and our basic objective will be to destroy Israel." Again, on May 26, 1967, Haykal wrote in *Al Ahram,* the official Egyptian newspaper: "I believe an armed clash between the UAR and Israel is inevitable." He relates how the United Nations Emergency Force was compelled to withdraw and how the Egyptian armed forces began occupying the border positions. This was followed by the advance on Sharm el-Sheik, the entrance to the Gulf of Aqaba. An order was issued to close the Gulf of Aqaba to Israeli shipping and to strategic goods for Israel, even if transported aboard non-Israeli ships. The results, says the author, were tangible: The Israeli plan against Syria collapsed and "it achieved another longed for and precious objective: the return of the armed forces to direct confrontation with Israel and the closing once again of the door to the Gulf of Aqaba in Israel's face. . . . I am confident that for many reasons, chiefly the psychological, Israel cannot accept or remain indifferent to what has taken place . . . Israel has to reply now. It has to deal a blow . . . Israel has no alternative but to use arms if it wants to exercise power."

In retrospect, Nasser, in a speech delivered at the University of Cairo on July 23, 1967, declared: "On 23rd May we announced the closure of the Gulf of Aqaba to Israeli ships. Then came the political changes in Israel at the beginning of June. As we followed what was going on there, the probability of war became 100 percent . . . I expected the aggression to take place on Monday 5, June, and the first blow to be struck at our airforce."

In his speech at the special Assembly of the United Nations on June 19, 1967, Abba Eban reiterated that "blockades have traditionally been regarded, in the pre-Charter parlance, as acts of war. To blockade, after all, is to attempt strangulation — and sovereign states are entitled not to have their states strangled. The blockade is by definition an act of war, imposed and enforced through violence. Never in history have blockade and peace existed side by side. From May 24 onward, the question of who started the war or fired the first shot became momentously irrelevant."

The Gulf of Aqaba is indeed an international waterway by geographic position and by the law of the sea. The Gulf is 100 miles long, lies to the east of the Gulf of Suez, running parallel to it, along the shores of the Sinai desert. Its coastline of 230 miles is shared by *four* countries — Egypt, Israel, Jordan, and Saudi Arabia. Quite obviously it is an international waterway.

The Gulf of Aqaba is approached from the south through

a channel which is three nautical miles wide, passing between the islands of Teiran and Sanafir. The status of these islands is undetermined but in April 1957 Saudi Arabia made a formal claim to them.

Leading maritime powers of the world have made it very clear that the Gulf of Aqaba is an international waterway. (The United Nations Security Council repeatedly called upon the Egyptian government to end its blockade in the Suez Canal and the Gulf of Aqaba.) According to international law, "The Gulfs and Bays enclosed by the land of more than one littoral state, however narrow their entrance may be, are non-territorial." These principles were reaffirmed in 1949 in the International Court of Justice. On January 15, 1957, the General Secretary of the United Nations said: "The international significance of the Gulf of Aqaba may be considered to justify the right of innocent passage through the Straits of Teiran and the Gulf in accordance with recognized rules of international law." The area was captured by Israel in 1956 and after the armistice it was occupied by the U.N. emergency force, till the UAR or Nasser asked them to leave. This was certainly an act of war and the actual outbreak of an armed conflict was only a matter of time.

The blockade may in part be due to economic reasons. The Israeli port of Elath connects by rail and road with Beer-sheba and Haifa on the Mediterranean, 150 miles away. The construction of a pipeline from Elath to the Mediterranean has been completed. This means severe competition to the Suez Canal and may well explain the blockade by Arab powers of the Gulf of Aqaba from 1949 to 1956.

It should not be overlooked that the Six-Day War had its roots in a local dispute, but would never have taken place without massive Soviet arms shipments to the UAR, Syria, Algeria, and Iraq.

The campaigns and the outcome of the Six-Day War are well known. The Israeli death toll was 759. According to Yizhak Rabin "these soldiers were carried over by spiritual values, deep spiritual resources, far more than by their weapons or their technique of warfare."

Arab casualties were extremely high. Jordan may have lost as many as 15,000 killed, Syrian casualties mounted to 5,000, Egypt's losses were catastrophic — and the worst of the existing problems have only been intensified. Mutual distrust has increased, additional refugees crowd the camps, economic losses are gigantic, the arms race devours millions of dollars and the stage is set for "the next round."

WHAT IS A JEW?

If the Israeli Declaration of Independence mentions "the right of the Jewish people to national restoration in their land" and emphasizes "the historical connection between the Jewish people and the land of Israel," it may come as a shock to discover that the question "What is a Jew?" is not answered with any degree of unanimity by the Jewish people themselves.

According to the dictionary, a Jew is

—a member of the tribe of Judah;
—an Israelite;
—a member of a nation existing in Palestine from the sixth century B.C. to the first century A.D.;
—one whose religion is Judaism.

The same authority defines a Hebrew as

—a member of or a descendant from one of a group of northern Semitic peoples including the Israelites; especially an Israelite;
—the Semitic language of the ancient Hebrews.

Obviously an Israeli is a native or an inhabitant of the republic of Israel.

The question "Who is a Jew?" is very complex. At one point Paul expressed the thought that "he is not a real Jew who is one outwardly, nor is true circumcision something external and physical. He is a Jew who is one inwardly, and real circumcision is a matter of the heart, spiritual and not literal" (Rom. 2:28, 29). Elsewhere, however, he adopts a different viewpoint and speaks of those who are "Jews by birth" (Gal. 2:15).

The word Jew is derived from Judah, son of Jacob. At first Judah was the name of a tribe. Later it became the political name by which the southern kingdom was known. Occasionally the word Israel was even used for the southern kingdom because it was a more spiritual designation, transcending the political "house of Judah" or "province of Judah." Israel designated the people of God regardless of politics and geography. After the collapse of the northern kingdom and the return from exile Israelite and Jew are used almost interchangeably.

Israel was used as a covenant name to designate all the descendants of Jacob. After the division of the kingdom the word was filled with political content to designate the northern kingdom (but still used in the higher sense as well). After the captivity, Jew and Israelite were used interchangeably, not only to refer to a member of the Jewish state or an inhabitant of Judea, but also to speak of a member of this people. The decisive characteristic was religious. A Jew or an Israelite was a worshiper of the one true God, a member of the chosen people.

In the following centuries the word Jew was largely used by non-Jews to speak of the chosen nation or by Jews when dealing with non-Jews. Israel is a higher designation, not normally used by non-Jews. Finally, the word Hebrew was perhaps not so much the name of a people as a descriptive term concerning the social position of the bearer. The original reference may be to nomads moving into civilization. It is generally used by strangers as a term for Israel. Obviously, the reference is frequently to the language spoken by the Jews.

As long as Jews were essentially religious the problem of definition was nonexistent. There was a time when Jews formed a cohesive community linked by the precepts of the oral and written law. Gradually, more and more, "Jews" became nonreligious. Are they still to be considered Jews? Is it a matter of religion, culture, nationality, language, or race?

- —It can hardly be a matter of religion because this definition of Jewishness would exclude the majority of Jews;
- —they no longer share a common culture. The cultural gap between the Yemenite and the U.S. Jew is enormous;
- —nationality is difficult to define. What constitutes a nation? What about those outside of Israel?
- —language is hardly a unifying factor. The majority of Jews do not know Hebrew;
- —the question of race is probably a matter of definition. Is there a Jewish race? If the racial aspect is the point of unity, what about the possibility of conversion to Judaism or from Judaism to another faith? These questions have agitated Israel and made headlines in Jewish communities across the world.

According to the Halakha, i.e., the body of religious law, a Jew is someone who has a Jewish mother. This definition has generally been accepted by religious and secular Jews, by the Orthodox, Conservative, and Reformed branches of Judaism. The idea is based on Deut. 7:3, 4: "You shall not make marriages with them, giving your daughters to their sons or taking their daughters for your sons. For they would turn away your sons from following me, to serve other gods." More literally, verse 4 reads, "for he would turn away your sons from following me." According to the rabbinical interpretation, *he,* i.e., the Gentile husband of your daughter, *will turn away your son,* i.e., the child of that union, *from following me.* Therefore, concluded the Rabbis, the child of a Gentile father and of a Jewish mother is Jewish, since only a Jew could be tempted to apostasy. On the other hand, the child of a Gentile mother and of a Jewish father is not Jewish. They also emphasize the fact that it says "your sons" so that the child of the Gentile father ("he") and a Jewish mother is recognized as belonging to the Jewish family.

Quite recently the Israeli Supreme Court made history by ruling that the child of a Jewish father and a non-Jewish mother may be registered as Jewish by nationality. At issue was the technical question whether the government can use the Halakha or ancient law to define the nationality. The answer of the Supreme Court was negative.

Under Israeli law, all residents are required to be listed in the population registry by nationality — either as Jewish, Arab, foreign or other. The new viewpoint of the Supreme Court does not alter the religious definition of Jewishness. The Supreme Court simply endorsed a national or cultural definition, thereby introducing a totally new element. This decision did not go unchallenged. The Israeli cabinet pressed for legislation to annul the Supreme Court's verdict. The cabinet backed two new laws. One stipulates that government registrars can accept as Jewish nationals only persons born to Jewish mothers or converted to Judaism (the traditional rule). The other law grants automatic Israeli citizenship to members of an immigrant family in which one spouse is Jewish. The vote of the nine Supreme Court judges was split 5 to 4, symbolic of the potential split the verdict might produce in the nation.

This recent ruling is extremely important in relation to immigration. Many Russian Jews, especially, are of mixed parentage and since a non-Jew does not enjoy the same privileges as a Jewish immigrant, Russian immigrants would suffer discrimination. This is why the cabinet backed the law that would grant automatic Israeli *citizenship* even though only one spouse might be Jewish.

There is a political aspect to the question. Critics of Israel have maintained that Israel is a theocratic state, racist in nature. It is true that a non-Jew cannot serve in the army, nor reach a high government position. He cannot marry a Jewish woman in Israel. Mixed marriages cannot be legalized. This seems paradoxical. Indeed, outside of Israel the existence and security of Jews depends on the concept of a pluralistic society, whereas inside of the land many embrace the vision of a Jewish state.

In June of 1970 the Chief Rabbinate made it clear that it does not recognize as a Jew a person who has been converted in any manner other than the Orthodox. The Rabbinate stressed the point that the population registry employees are forbidden by Jewish law to list as Jewish converts those who have not been converted according to *halacha,* i.e., the Jewish religious code.

Many other definitions of Jewishness have been suggested. David ben-Gurion contended that anyone who wished to be considered a Jew should be accepted as such. At this point the concept was totally divorced from race or the accident of birth.

The survival of the Jews across the centuries was not due to a common territory nor a common language and not even a common religion — unless the definition of religion is broadened considerably, including not only religious acts and convictions but behavior patterns and customs. Jewishness would then lower to the level of culture. This would enable the vast number of non-religious Jews to claim Jewishness in all good conscience, but the question immediately arises whether such a cultural bond really existed. Is there a real link of this nature between a Jew from Iraq and Germany, from Morocco and the United States?

There does not seem to be any valid reason why an Israeli citizen could not be an Arab by nationality and a Muslim by religion. The orthodox object that the distinction between religion and nationality cannot be accepted in Israel, but it is of course valid for Jews outside of the land of Promise.

It is interesting that anti-Semites have never found it difficult to determine Jewishness — regardless of the criteria employed. But it is hardly rational for Israel to leave the determination in the hands of non-Jews.

It has been suggested that self-identification is sufficient. Is it not enough to say: I am a Jew, I identify with the Jewish people? But is it really enough for an Arab to say: I am an American, or I am a Christian, to settle the question? Are there no objective standards?

If Jewishness is determined by birth (a Jewish mother) can it ever be lost? What about the notorious case of Brother Daniel, a convert to Catholicism, who became a monk and was not accepted as a Jew in Israel?

Actually, when a survey was conducted in Israel, 59 percent of those who were asked, "Who is a Jew?" gave varying answers such as "those who consider themselves to be Jews" or "those who live in Israel and identify with the State." Only 19 percent gave an answer in accordance with ancient rabbinical law.

The more recent debate centering on the Shalit case has only brought the problem into sharper focus. It is anticipated that this is the last time that children of a non-Jewish mother will be registered as Jewish, as legislation will make Jewish religious law the criterion for Interior Ministry registrations. Even after the ruling of the Supreme Court, the problem of mixed marriage has not been resolved, because in matters of marriage, the state is not the master; all such regulations are exclusively religious.

A definition of "Jew" is needed in connection with the law of return, otherwise it is impossible to know who is entitled to immigrate into Israel. The Supreme Court touched only on the question of nationality. But the word "nationality" which appears on Israeli identity cards has no clearly defined meaning. Since it is important for the government to know if a person is Jewish or Arab they are unwilling to strike the question from the identity card.

A nation is usually defined by a territorial limit and a common sovereignty. There are other ways of looking at it. A nation can coincide with the state and often does. On the other hand, there can be more than one nation inside of a sovereign state. Looking for common factors to determine a nation complicates the problem. Language is not necessarily a common factor. In Switzerland four languages are spoken. Size is not related to the issue since tiny states are as much a nation as the United States. Even boundaries are not an ultimate criterion since a national group can overflow state boundaries. This, in fact, is frequently the case in Africa, not to mention the millions of Chinese who live outside of mainland China. Religion is hardly a common bond, and so one may have to fall back on the concept of a common culture, be this idea ever so abstract. In other words, common habits, common traditions, customs, and a desire to live together as a separate entity would constitute a nation. To what extent this applies to Israel in the past and in what measure this is relevant today are moot questions.

From the standpoint of Scripture the unique dimension of the Jewish nation is rooted in a concrete relationship to God. When this covenant is disregarded the Jew sinks to the level of a pagan for all practical purposes and loses his uniqueness. (Hosea 1:8, 9; 2:23; cf. 1 Pet. 2:10). From the biblical perspective it is not really sufficient to limit the concept of Jewishness to descent from a Jewish mother. In this connection the Shalit case is particularly interesting because they are both atheists.

As might be expected the national religious party is determined to enact a law which would define a Jew according to Halakha. Others would like to bypass the question of nationality and omit it from the registration rolls. What is finally at stake is the question whether the state of Israel is simply a new independent nation similar to the many other new nations which have emerged over the last two decades, or whether there is actually a return to the land of an ancient nation, reestablishing herself in a homeland. Although the Balfour Declaration and a few other documents favor the latter view, the issue is by no means settled.

Other practical considerations are related to life in Israel. For instance, employment of labor on the Sabbath has always been banned, except for certain vital services specially licensed by the Labor Ministry. Orthodox Jews have tried to impose the same ban on self-employed people. This was finally achieved and the Sabbath law now prohibits self-employed businessmen, artisans and factory owners from working in their premises on the Sabbath. An exception is made for filling stations. At one point, the problem of a public swimming pool which was open on the Sabbath in Jerusalem became a national issue. According to the Talmud it is forbidden to bathe the whole body in hot water on the Sabbath. Swimming is forbidden in a river, but scholars have believed that it is permitted in a swimming pool, provided the latter has a rim around the edge. Incidentally, the tennis courts of the University are available for play on Saturday and this has never become a public issue. Although buses are generally not in use, they continue to run from Haifa to Mount Carmel and from Tel Aviv to Herzliya. Elsewhere only taxis are available, since all public transportation is at a standstill. El Al flights are not permitted out of the International airport.

Since many of the immigrants who arrived in Israel were not married according to Jewish law or have non-Jewish wives, many practical problems arose. Again when the Egyptians sank the destroyer Elath on October 21, 1967, it took a special announcement of the Chief Rabbi of Israel's defense forces to pronounce the sixteen sailors dead. Under Jewish religious law, there is no status of people being "presumed dead." In other words, the wife of such a man may not remarry unless his body is found or witnesses vouch for his death, or a competent religious authority decides that he may be declared dead because of the circumstances of his disappearance. The latter course was adopted so that the widows could remarry. Not long ago the Haifa Rabbinical Court complied with the request of a local couple married for fourteen years that the husband should be allowed to marry a second wife, so that he may have children.

One wonders how long the non-religious Jew will find life under religious law tolerable. It is not difficult to foresee that once the political situation with Israel's neighbors has stabilized, serious internal crises will develop.

Much is at stake, then, in the definition of Jewishness. If a religious and Orthodox view prevails indefinitely, it is to be expected that their viewpoint will gain more and more influence in national affairs. Already many of the ancient laws are enforced upon citizens who are hardly religious. This trend could continue and be amplified. Right now Israel has too many external problems to give serious consideration to these issues, but these fundamental problems have not been resolved in the young State of Israel. On the other hand, if another definition than the ancient Orthodox formula were adopted to define a Jew, it might sap the foundations of national life. Historic continuity might be discarded in favor of a different concept and by the same token, the idea of a "return" would have to be abandoned. The theological and practical impasse is considerable. The interpenetration of church and state is indeed a dilemma, tends to generate intolerance, and to limit individual freedom. As Christians we must give serious consideration to the precarious position of the Israeli Christians and the Arab Christians under the current laws governing the land and the life of Israel.

The dilemma of contemporary Jews — the problem "Who is a Jew?" — is due to the fact that the great majority has lost a dynamic relationship with God. It is absurd to speak of a chosen nation and to deny God who performed the choice. If a Jew is by definition a member of the chosen people it is difficult, not to say impossible, to conceive of a Jewish atheist who clings to his Jewishness (whatever that may be) while he denies God. It is also irrational to cling to the ancient promises of God and yet to consign the book of Genesis to the realm of legend. Historic claims can hardly be validated by legends. In other words, liberal Jewish theology cannot seriously speak of God's choice nor make specific claims to the land. On the other hand, Orthodox Jews have overlaid the teaching of the Old Testament by Talmudic and traditional interpretation. The net result is a broad ignorance of the Old Testament coupled with a rigid adherence to Jewish law and customs. It is indeed difficult to speak of a Return to the land — and to spell return with a capital R — while harboring doubt about Jewish identity. From a purely Jewish perspective these questions must be exceedingly troubling and vexing. It is not sufficient to exploit Scripture for political purposes and to speak rhetorically of the inalienable connection between the Jew and the land while essentially denying the validity of the Old Testament or the inspiration of the prophets.

From a Christian perspective it is not difficult to see the hand of God at work, accomplishing his sovereign purposes regardless of the attitude of man. Even as he uses godless nations such as the Assyrians or Babylonians to accomplish his purposes, so he can use Israel to achieve his plans. As in the days of old God's sovereignty did not cancel man's responsibility and even as God punished the nations although they unwittingly fulfilled his purposes, so it is today. Although the return of Israel to the land does fulfill God's purposes it does not justify every action of the Israeli government nor cancel their responsibility. It is true that the Balfour Declaration and subsequent documents of the League of Nations and of the United Nations have recognized the historic link between the Jew and Palestine, but this in itself does not give title to the land. It is questionable whether an international body such as the United Nations or the League of Nations or for that matter whether a Western power such as Great Britain has a right to partition the land — be it Israel or any other part of the world. Britain had defeated Turkey and exercized sovereignty over Palestine. They used their political prerogatives and were of course perfectly free to dispose of the conquered territory as they pleased.

It should then be recognized that the presence of Israel today is essentially due to conquest, be it British or Israeli. It will not do to veil this fact by frequent quotation of the prophets or by speaking of historic rights. The Jews are firmly established in the land and have been recognized not only on a de facto basis but also on a de jure basis. Their sovereignty and national existence is recognized and guaranteed by most of the other nations of the world. Most nations exist today because at one time the territory they now occupy was conquered. Israel is hardly an exception to the rule. To claim divine sanction for the conquest is hardly legitimate for those who deny the reality of God and the inspiration of the promises. It does make sense for Christians to recognize God's sovereignty at work in the historic circumstances of our generation. It goes without saying that God's sovereignty is exercised over all nations, but it is more difficult for the Christian to speak about it with any degree of certainty when no indications are given in Scripture as to God's plans or purposes. In connection with Israel God has made specific commitments and the fulfillment of these is becoming increasingly evident in the last few decades.

It is sad that Israel has not only failed to maintain the ancient relationship with God but also refused to enter into the new relationship which was predicted by Jeremiah. The heart of the new covenant would be the forgiveness of sin based on a genuine knowledge of God, internalization of the law in contrast with the law written on tables of stone (Jer. 31:31-34). It remains true then as Paul put it, that the true Jew is one who is circumcized inwardly and who has a living, dynamic relationship with God through the Messiah, Jesus Christ.

ISRAELI POPULATION

There have always been a few Jews in Palestine, but in 1882 when Zionism began as a movement there were only about 24,000 Jews in the land. At the turn of the century the area now occupied by the State of Israel was an integral part of the Arab world. The Jewish population constituted a minority of less than 50,000 persons.

In 1922, when the first modern census was taken in Palestine, there were 752,000 inhabitants of whom about 11 percent or 84,000 were Jews. By 1931 there were 175,000 Jewish inhabitants. Gradually the proportion of the Jewish population increased so that by March 1947, it reached 32 percent. One year later, when Israel was established as an independent nation on May 15, 1948, the proportion of Jews in the population of that portion of Palestine which was incorporated into the State of Israel was about 51 percent or 650,000. Obviously the partition plan of the United Nations had envisioned a Jewish state, containing a Jewish majority of 60 percent, but one that would also include an Arab minority of 40 percent.

By 1952, as a result of further Jewish immigration and Arab exodus, the proportion of Jews in Israel was almost 90 percent or 1,421,000. This extraordinary growth was largely due to immigration which had its peak in 1948-49 accounting for 92 percent of the population growth. The crude rate of natural increase is also relatively high and has rarely fallen below 20 per 1,000 inhabitants. At the same time, the death rate of the Jewish population is one of the lowest in the world. The high natural increase is largely due to the immigrants from surrounding Asian nations and North Africa whose fertility rates are higher than those of Jews who came from Europe.

Although many people assume that most of the Jewish population lives in kibbutzim or collective settlements, the rural population is small. When the first Israeli census was taken in 1948, the percentage of urban population was almost 84. The percentage has dropped, but most people live in urban areas.

Obviously, immigration has played a key role in the settlement of the land. The first large wave came between 1924 and 1926, followed by an even larger wave between 1933 and 1939, at which point the British issued the White Paper limiting all subsequent Jewish immigration to Palestine to 75,000 for the next five years. This policy, coupled with the events of World War II, reduced immigration tremendously. Once established as a sovereign state, Israel encouraged immigration and an enormous flow arrived between 1948 and 1951, at times at a rate as high as 30,000 per month. More recently a sharp decline has set in. For instance, in 1966 only 12,000 Jewish immigrants came to Israel.

Although Jewish immigration is regarded as "large-scale," this is true only by comparison with the Jewish population of Israel, but certainly not in comparison to international migrations elsewhere. From the Arab viewpoint it is important to recall that in 1917, at the time of the Balfour Declaration which guaranteed "a national home for the Jewish people" in Palestine, the Jews constituted less than 10 percent of the total population. The problem of population is an extremely important factor in Israel because

—of the large minority of Arabs living in Israel and the occupied territories;

—of the vast Arab population surrounding Israel;

—of the intricate refugee problem.

As to the first point, according to the latest statistics, the population of Israel has risen to 2,919,000, including 422,-000 non-Jews (70,000 of them in East Jerusalem). The Jewish population increased by 2.5 percent whereas the non-Jewish population increased by 3.8 percent. Two-thirds of the growth of the Jewish population stems from natural increase. Obviously, immigration has really slowed down. A Jewish newspaper recently stated that 1967 was a good year for French emigration to the Jewish state because one thousand people left France to settle in Israel. Approximately 6,000 to 8,000 are expected in 1969. But large scale immigration can no longer be expected. The USSR is unwilling to release the many Jews in the Soviet Union and American Jews have shown no inclination to go to Jerusalem since most of them enjoy a higher living standard in the United States.

Given the above figures, the Arab population of Israel now constitutes 14 percent of the total. In addition, there are approximately one million Arabs who live in the West Bank and the Gaza Strip. If these territories and their inhabitants were incorporated into Israel, the total Arab population would rise to 40 percent. One might almost say that the military victory could become a demographic catastrophe. Yet, one should also recall that the original partition plan of the United Nations envisioned a state which would be bi-racial, since Jews would only have constituted 60 percent of the total population. Perhaps this would be a most useful corrective to the Jewish state undoubtedly compelling a revision of certain prevailing attitudes.

These demographic factors have probably inspired the political proposal to establish the West Bank as a federated or semi-autonomous Arab state with economic ties to Israel. To counterbalance this large Arab segment of the population, Jewish immigration is desperately needed. Yet at the same time, as has just been pointed out, the reservoir is well-nigh exhausted. In spite of the ardent propaganda of devoted Zionists, immigration has slowed down to a trickle. The unrest in the Middle East is not conducive to increasing immigration.

It is important to recall that Israeli casualties have been relatively high. It is true that only 700 Israelis died in the June War, but it is a relatively high percentage of a total population of 2.5 million people. The death of 700 Israelis would be the equivalent of the death of 60,000 Americans. In the two years subsequent to the June War, Israel lost another 700 dead so that the total casualties would be the equivalent to 120,000 Americans. In addition, there are of course many wounded — but very few prisoners. These population factors have encouraged the Arab nations to attempt a war of attrition which they are sure to win. In May 1970 casualties reached the highest peak since the June War. A total of 43 soldiers and 18 civilians were killed and 105 soldiers and 31 civilians, wounded.

If Israel were to incorporate the occupied areas, thereby automatically increasing the percentage of the Arab population, one could almost predict that within twenty years the Arabs would be the majority in Israel since they have a higher birth rate.

From the Christian standpoint it is important to recall that far more Christians now live under Israeli rule than previous to the June War since many Palestinians are Christians. In fact, as many as 10 percent had embraced some form of Christian teaching and the events in the Middle East have certainly been a grave setback for the Church. Through the exodus of refugees and the migration of people church life has been seriously disrupted.

Israel is surrounded by a sea of Arabs. According to the latest census, the total population of Iran, Iraq, Jordan, Kuwait, Lebanon, Saudi Arabia, Syria, UAR, and Yemen comes to 118,000,000 people. If Algeria, Libya, Morocco, Sudan, and Tunisia are added the total comes to 168,000,-000. All these figures include the Palestine refugees. Because the entire Middle Eastern atmosphere is envenomed by the refugee problem, it is essential to pay particular attention to the displaced Palestinians. This is true not only for political or economic reasons, but also from a purely Christian and humanitarian standpoint.

THE REFUGEES

When the men of Hezekiah penned the ancient proverb "Like a bird that strays from its nest, is a man who strays from his home" (Prov. 27:8), they were certainly not thinking of the millions who have been displaced since World War II. Chinese are crowding Hong Kong, Cubans find refuge in Miami, millions are left homeless in Africa. Over seven million Hindus fled Pakistan for India and even more Muslims left India for Pakistan. Many Arab refugees have languished in camps for over twenty years, although forty million refugees have been resettled since World War II. Unfortunately the political dimensions of the Arab refugee problem have dominated the human aspect. The United Nations Relief and Works Agency (UNRWA) has spent about six hundred million dollars of which two-thirds has been contributed by the United States. The Soviet Union has not contributed to the fund. UNRWA has only been able to provide minimal subsistence to a growing number on the rolls. The problem has been perpetuated rather than solved. The 45,000 Arabs in UNRWA administration have a vested interest in maintaining the bureaucracy.

Although no one knows the exact number, when the 1948-49 firing ended, refugees totaled somewhere between 700,000 and 800,000. Because of arguments and discrepancies it may be important to document this figure to some extent. The settled non-Jewish population as of December 31, 1946, in territory held by the Israeli army on May 1, 1949, may be taken to have been 736,000. The bedouin population may be taken to have been 105,000. The natural increase from December 31, 1946, to May 15, 1948, may be estimated at about 40,000. The net out-migration of the non-Jewish population between January 1, 1947, and May 15, 1948, may be taken to have been about 250,000. These figures lead to an estimate of 630,000 non-Jews in Israel on May 15, 1948.*

The reason for the out-migration of so many Arabs before Israeli independence is due to the chaotic situation which preceded May 15, 1948. The withdrawal of the British initiated a period of strife and bloodshed. The occasional acts of terrorism precipitated the exodus of many Arabs. Conservative Jewish sources will admit to approximately 600,000 Arab refugees who fled Palestine in 1947-49, and concede that they could currently number 1,330,-000.** These initial refugees are often called "old" refugees in order to distinguish them from those who fled later. At one point the Israeli government offered to the Conciliation Commission to permit the return of 100,000 refugees, subject to certain conditions, one of which was that Israel "reserve the right to resettle the repatriated refugees in specific locations, in order to ensure that their reinstallation would fit into the general plan of Israel's economic development." The proposal was considered unsatisfactory and was rejected.

By now there are *at least* 1,300,000 on the UNRWA rolls, partly through the addition of new refugees due to subsequent wars and partly through natural increase. It is well known that every agency providing welfare assistance

---

*These statistics are based on *Israel: Jewish Population and Immigration,* published by the U.S. Department of Commerce, Bureau of the Census, p. 57.
***A Case for Israel* by Frank Gervasi.

has difficulty with eligibility, and has to struggle constantly to exclude those who are not eligible. Since the beginning of this operation, UNRWA has removed 300,000 names from the rolls, either because of death or false registration or other reasons. Then again, UNRWA has suspended the eligibility of an accumulative total of 355,000 persons who were absent from the territory or who had been able to obtain a family income of more than $40.00 per month. It is also true that many of these later lost their income or returned from absence so that the net decrease was only 210,-000.

After the events of June 1967, the distinction between old and new refugees came into being, which has confused the issue even more. As a result of the last war there are at least 250,000 additional Arab refugees who previously lived in the West Bank or the Golan Heights. Most of them — perhaps as many as 200,000 — fled to Jordan. Adding those from other areas, the June War produced about 225,000 additional Arab refugees.

Where are the refugees today? Egypt had segregated its refugees in the Gaza Strip across the Sinai desert, away from its own population centers. The population of the Gaza Strip before the June War was estimated at 450,000 of whom 320,000 were refugees of the 1948 conflict. The UNRWA census listed 315,000 refugees in this Strip; Israeli authorities claimed that the rolls were padded and that the true figure probably was close to 270,000. These people were never granted Egyptian citizenship and did not enjoy freedom of movement. They were subject to Egyptian military law.

Syria would have had ample room for the 70,000 or so who fled to it. *Lebanon* faced a serious problem when over 80,000 refugees arrived. Their absorption would disrupt the very delicate balance between Christians and Muslims on which the country's political existence is based.

Jordan was perhaps glad to accept its refugees as additional subjects to an otherwise minuscule population. Almost 40 percent of the population of Jordan consists of refugees. The total comes to about 400,000 of which 175,-000 arrived since the June War. In July 1967, Israel announced that she would allow the return of the refugees from the last conflict. This led to prolonged negotiations between the International Committee of the Red Cross and the governments of Israel and Jordan. Refugees who had crossed over to the East Bank of Jordan between June 5 and July 4, 1967, and whose applications were approved by Israel, would be allowed to return to their homes. About 40,000 applications were submitted to Israel for the return of 150,-000 refugees. The number of applications approved and permits issued by Israel is stated on the Jordan side to be 5,122 relating to 18,236 persons and on the Israeli side to be 5,787 relating to 20,658 persons. In fact, the people who actually crossed the Jordan by August 31 numbered slightly over 14,000.

Everything connected with refugees has been the subject of innumerable debates. Were they compelled to flee or did they leave the country of their own volition? Could they have been absorbed into the various economies of the surrounding nations? Should they be allowed repatriation into Israel? Who carries the main burden of responsibility? Before considering some of these questions it is necessary to look over the situation of the Jews in Arab lands.

Remnants of the Jewish dispersion which began in 586 B.C. are scattered throughout the Arab world. Outside of Israel, the oldest Jewish communities are in Egypt and Iraq. The situation was tolerable across the centuries, although Jews were always treated as second-class citizens. They were respected as "people of the book." Many of them prospered and some even occupied eminent positions. The situation has altered radically in recent years.

Egypt: At the end of World War II there were approximately 80,000 Jews in Egypt. Only 5,000 were Egyptian citizens. About 40,000 were stateless, although they had lived in Egypt for generations. The rest were foreign nationals. After 1948, 20,000 Jews left Egypt, leaving their property behind. In 1956, during the Suez campaign, there were still 50,000 Jews in Egypt but they diminished rapidly so that less than 1,000 live in Egypt today. Many languish in prison. It is estimated that the Egyptian government seized $400,000,000 worth of Jewish property.

Tunisia: There are currently 8,000 Jews in Tunisia who live in relative quiet.

Algeria: Only between 1,000 and 2,000 Jews remain in Algeria.

Morocco: Under the enlightened rule of Hassan II, about 50,000 Jews are able to pursue normal communal activities. Back in 1950 some 200,000 lived in Morocco.

Lebanon: The situation has been quiet. The 7,000 Jews who live there are mostly domiciled in Beirut. Three synagogues function, as well as one hospital.

Iraq: In the early '50s some 120,000 Jewish people migrated to Israel in Operation Ezra and Nehemiah. Only 7,000 remained in Iraq. The number is now down to 2,500. They live under a reign of terror and are virtually prisoners. They are not allowed to leave their homes, have no passports, their telephones have been confiscated, they are not permitted to sell property, and they remain under constant surveillance.

Syria: Back in 1947 there were 14,000 Jews in Syria, mostly in Aleppo and Damascus. In 1949 about 5,000 left Syria, fleeing by way of Lebanon, which resisted Syrian demands that they be returned. Today only 4,000 are left and these are deprived of basic human rights. A Jewish school is still open in Damascus with an enrollment of 300 students.

Libya: Most of the 4,000 Jews in Libya left after the June War. Many are imprisoned and less than 1,000 are now left in Libya.

Another very important factor has to be taken into consideration — the Arab population of Israel. During the Six-Day War there were 336,000 Arabs living in Israel. There was not a single act of sabotage. These Arabs are full Israeli citizens. In terms of education and economy they are considerably better off than most of their brethren across the Middle East. Their material conditions are constantly improving, but they are conscious of the lack of economic equality with the country's Jews. This is partly due to the fact that those who stayed behind in 1948 were largely unlettered, non-urban Arabs. It was under the Premiership of Eli Eshkol that restrictions were gradually removed. Today Israeli Arabs enjoy full citizenship with all its rights and responsibilities except one — they are not required to serve in the armed forces. Seven Arabs are members of the Knesset. The per capita income of the Israeli Arabs is $850.00 a year over against $200.00 for the Arabs who live on the West Bank and came under Israeli control after the June War. On the other hand, the overall Israeli per capita income is $1,200.00 per year.

It is a post-war fact that hundreds of thousands of Arab refugees live under Israeli control. The Gaza Strip can hardly provide a self-supporting economy for the people in that area. To solve the economic problem, about half of them would have to be transferred to other areas. Resettlement costs would be enormous.

It has often been attempted to pinpoint the responsibility for the plight of the refugees on specific circumstances or official attitudes.

From the *Jewish* viewpoint the Arab governments invaded Israel in 1948 and thereby created the problem. Seen from this angle the world community has the right to claim the assistance of the Arab nations to settle the problem. Besides, it is pointed out that the Arabs have both the land and the resources so they could easily liberate the refugees from their plight. In addition, the Jews point out that they have received 450,000 refugees from Arab lands who arrived in Palestine totally destitute. Should it not be easy for the Arab nations to take care of the refugees who speak the same language, have religious ties, and share the same social background? As far as Israel is concerned, repatriation is almost impossible. So many refugees could not possibly be absorbed into the Israeli economy. Cheap Arab labor would be poured into the economy and exert pressure on wages. The security risks would be enormous. Finally, the Israelis point to the fact that more than half of the refugees are under fifteen years of age which means that when Israel was established they were not even alive — so that one can hardly speak of repatriation.

Over against this the *Arabs* hold that the refugees were literally driven into exile. They stressed the fact that Palestinians fled because of Jewish terrorism and forced expulsion. Panic resulted from rumors regarding real or alleged acts of Jewish terrorism, especially after the famous massacre which took place at Dier Yassin on April 9, 1948, in which 300 persons perished. The Arabs also point out that along with independence Israel seized 23 percent more territory than was allotted to her in the 1947 U.N. partition plan. As someone pointed out, those German Jews who welcomed the opportunity to return to Germany could hardly have been persuaded that the return of Germans from Czechoslovakia would be a fair exchange. Similarly, the coming of Jews from Arab lands to Israel is hardly relevant to the refugee problem. Arabs never tire of pointing out that the land was occupied, but that Zionists have never recognized this fact in their official publication. The Arab in Palestine was the invisible man, from the standpoint of Zionism.

It would be useless to enumerate all the arguments pro and con. That many Arabs fled because of acts of terrorism, especially perpetrated by the Stern Gang and the Irgun, cannot be denied. That rumors exaggerated the significance of terrorist acts is undeniable. On the other hand, that the mayor of Haifa and other responsible Jewish leaders urged the Arabs not to leave is also documented. After all, no Arab government ordered the Palestinians to leave during the Six-Day War, but 150,000 Arabs fled from the West Bank to the East Bank. To analyze their reasons, to dissect their motivation, to distinguish the political from the psychological and the emotional from the financial is hardly relevant. Many were undoubtedly afraid to be cut off from their families and from the paychecks coming from Kuwait and other areas where relatives had found employment. So many different factors come into play that each side can claim a certain number of reasons and feel perfectly justified. Unfortunately the problem has become political and the humanitarian aspects are largely overlooked. The issue of the refugees should not be exploited for propaganda purposes. Maintaining them in camps and restricted areas makes the recruiting of volunteers for guerrilla activities much easier. Besides, absorption of the refugees into Arab economies would either resolve the Palestinian problem or create an economic imbalance, alternatives which are perhaps equally unpleasant to the Arab nations.

On the other hand, Jewish responsibility cannot be overlooked. They, of all people, should know what it means to be refugees. Many Arab refugees should be given the choice of repatriation in Israel or resettlement in Arab countries. In the latter case, some compensation should be received from Israel. It would be possible to settle many in the West Bank but this plan is usually rejected because Israelis feel that suitable land available should be reserved for Jewish settlements.

Actually, many Jews are afraid to accept sole responsibility for *any* group of Arab refugees lest they find themselves automatically called upon to settle *all* refugees within their borders, irrespective of political, economic, defense, or national considerations.

A short time after assuming the Premiership, Mrs. Meir asked for a concrete plan for the settlement of Arab refugees. A detailed proposal was submitted for settling 10,000 families at El Arish. The idea is that this settlement could provide a model which would serve as a token of Israel's good will and as an example of how the issue could be tackled. The idea is to provide a livelihood for 10,000 earners of a population of 50,000. About 3,000 would be engaged in farming, 2,000 in industry, and 5,000 in services and professions. The farmers would be accommodated in ten villages scattered over a relatively small area. Within less than ten years the farmers would be expected to reach the present Israeli agricultural level. The income would be expected to average about $200.00 per capita, which is better than the current $120.00 in the Gaza Strip. A political solution accompanied the plan which envisions the creation of a semi-autonomous region which would ultimately involve over 100,000 people.

Recent American proposals included the idea that Arab refugees from the 1948 war would be given a choice of repatriation to Israel or resettlement in Arab countries with compensation from Israel. The exact number to be repatriated would depend on Israeli-Jordanian negotiations. An International Commission would determine the choice of each refugee in returning to Israel. Since procedures would be lengthy, the proposal stated that the rest of the peace plan could be implemented before the refugee procedures are carried out.

One significant factor related to the refugee problem is the value of property left behind by the Palestinians. A global assessment was made in 1951 by the refugee office. As to immovable property, the estimate was based on the value of the land for "existing use." The refugee office excluded certain factors which had "forced up prices." Several complex yardsticks were used and in the end the assessment was approximately 100 million pounds sterling. As to movable property lost by the refugees, it was calculated to be slightly over 19 million Palestinian pounds or the equivalent of less than $60.00 per capita.

As might be expected, the Israeli government laid its hands upon lands, buildings, and property which had once belonged to the Palestinians. The Abandoned Areas Ordinances (1948) stipulated that the government could declare certain areas as "abandoned" and proceed to appropriate and confiscate the property. This was followed by the Cultivation of Waste Lands Regulations (1948). Waste land was defined as land not cultivated or not efficiently cultivated. Abandoned or absentee property was placed under the authority of the Custodian of Abandoned Property. By 1953, abandoned Arab property had been fully utilized. Repatriated Arab refugees were receiving land by renting it from the government. Meanwhile, 350 of the 370 settlements which had come into being since the establishment of the state were situated on abandoned property. The custodian owned 50,000 flats and 10,000 business premises. These would be sold to their present occupants at "prevailing prices" if the government approved this action. In fact, a recommendation to that effect had already been passed by the Knesset Finance Committee and only cabinet approval was necessary to begin the sales. By January of 1953, there were only 2.5 m dunams of agricultural land and 1 m dunams of arid land under the authority of the Custodian. Two-thirds of this land had already been transferred to the Jewish National Fund. In addition, there were only 100,000 dunams in urban areas which the Custodian would sell at the prevailing cost of land. Money accruing from these sales would go to the development authorities. Four dunams are approximately equal to one acre (*Jerusalem Post,* January 18, 1953).

As might well be expected it has been pointed out by Israeli authorities that Jews living in Arab nations left a great deal of property behind when they fled to Israel. At the same time, Israel is prepared to pay some compensation to the refugees and to help with the international settlement of the refugee question. Still, the property problem remains a very thorny question.

OCCUPIED TERRITORIES

The November 22, 1967, resolution of the U.N. Security Council called for:

—the withdrawal of Israeli armed forces from territories occupied in the June 1967 war; and

—termination of all claims or states of belligerency and respect for an acknowledgment of the sovereignty, territorial integrity, and political independence of every State in the area and their right to live in peace within secure and recognized boundaries free from threats or acts of force.

The resolution also affirms the necessity for guaranteeing freedom of navigation through international waterways in the area; for achieving a just settlement of the refugee problem; and for guaranteeing the territorial inviolability and political independence of every State in the area.

The Arab-Israeli conflict has been the topic of many Security Council resolutions, but they have largely remained ineffective, ignored either by the Israelis or the Arabs or both.

Since the Six-Day War Israel has occupied

—the Golan Heights;

—the Gaza Strip;

—the West Bank;
—the Sinai.

Special mention should also be made of Old Jerusalem.

From the military standpoint these areas represent a tremendous gain. Israeli farm settlements had been shelled for years by Syrian gunners from the Golan Heights. The Gaza Strip extended like a knife into Israel. The Sinai is an excellent buffer against Egyptian aggression and protects Israeli cities from UAR air raids. Finally, the borderline with Jordan has been shortened considerably, running along 70 miles instead of 180 miles and following the river Jordan instead of a twisted line across hills and scrub.

The political and demographic factors are not so positive. The occupied areas do not seem to enhance the Israeli bargaining position. The Israelis insist on direct negotiations leading to a signed peace treaty, and the Arabs insist with equal vehemence on the prior withdrawal of Israel from Arab-occupied territories.

Israeli views regarding the territories are manifold.

—*The Golan Heights*: There seems to be an almost unanimous agreement among politicians of all factions that Israel should keep the Golan Heights indefinitely. The mountain range to the north and northeast is considered Israel's natural frontier. The long years of shelling from the top of the Heights have not been forgotten. Even the late Prime Minister Eshkol stated in his famous *Newsweek* interview: "You know what happened on the Golan Heights before the war. Never again. Besides, these are not settlements, but military, agricultural posts." Actually, the Golan Heights are already under Israeli civil law. Also, the Jewish population has increased from nil to 10,000 since the conquest and fourteen kibbutzim or collective settlements have been set up. Israel is there to stay.

—*The Gaza Strip*: Some advocate self-government except in matters of internal or external security. Unfortunately, the area cannot possibly sustain the population living in the Gaza Strip. The lack of capital resources and the abundance of unskilled labor complicate the situation. The people compressed in the area have never enjoyed Egyptian citizenship. Their political status is uncertain. Their relationship to Egypt and Jordan is doubtful.

Some Israelis have suggested that Gaza become one element of a federation consisting of the Central area (Israel), the West Bank, Gaza, and perhaps a fourth region. Based on the present population, the Central Parliament would be composed of seventy-one representatives from the Central area, eighteen from the West Bank, and eleven from Gaza. Because of Jewish fears concerning the rapid natural increase of the Arab population and because of Arab concern over Jewish immigration, representation could be frozen at those levels for a long period. On the other hand, it would also appear that many Palestinians refuse to go along with such a plan unless the other Arab States sign a peace treaty and unless a free choice is given to all refugees to return to Palestine. Many do not want a Palestinian state and prefer union with Jordan.

—*The West Bank*: Aside from the federation plan just mentioned, which would also involve the West Bank, the so-called Allon plan has received much attention. The area would be turned over to the Arabs except for a strip of territory along the Jordan River. Israel would establish armed settlements on the commanding Judean heights west of the river to guard against infiltration. A corridor north of Jerusalem would connect the West Bank with Jordan. On the other hand, the people might prefer not to be related to the Hashemite kingdom

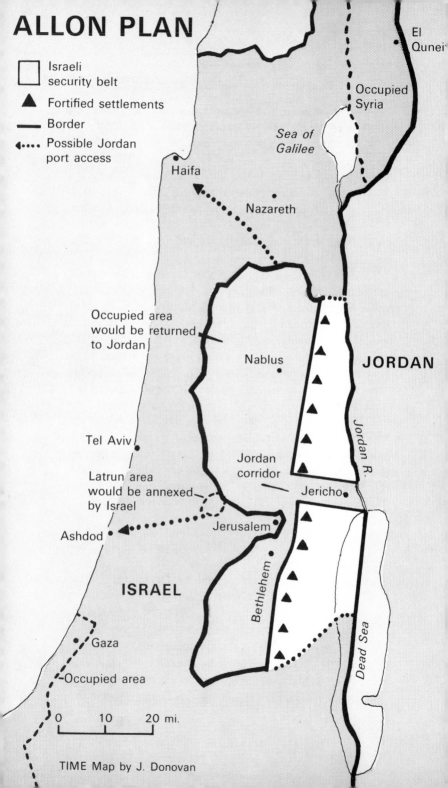

ALLON PLAN

- ☐ Israeli security belt
- ▲ Fortified settlements
- — Border
- ◀···· Possible Jordan port access

El Qunei

Occupied Syria

Sea of Galilee

Haifa

Nazareth

Occupied area would be returned to Jordan

Nablus

JORDAN

Tel Aviv

Jordan corridor

Jordan R.

Latrun area would be annexed by Israel

Jericho

Ashdod

Jerusalem

ISRAEL

Bethlehem

Gaza

Occupied area

Dead Sea

0   10   20 mi.

TIME Map by J. Donovan

of Jordan and opt for an independent Palestinian state.

—*The Sinai*: Some favor gradual withdrawal now, midway between the Suez Canal and the ancient borders; others like to keep the desert because it is a useful buffer zone and creates few internal problems since it is sparsely populated. It could also be used to resettle Arab refugees.

The Tiran Straits and Sharm-e-Sheikh represent special problems. As Moshe Dayan put it in his epoch-making speech (April 1969): "These straits lead only to us. They lead to Jordan too but it has no particular importance for them. But free sea passage to Elath for our trade and oil that comes through the Tiran Straits — this is a question of life and death for us.

These straits do not lead to any Egyptian port. The sole interest the Egyptians have on the isles and at Sharm-e-Sheikh is their capability to strangle us."

—*Old Jerusalem* is an issue charged with emotion. It was formally annexed by Israel regardless of U.N. resolutions and subsequent protests. On July 4, 1967, the United Nations called upon Israel to "cancel all measures taken to alter the status of Jerusalem, all such measures being regarded as legally void." Later, recalling resolutions 2253 and 2254 of July 4 and 14, 1967, and resolution 252 of May 21, 1968, concerning measures and actions by Israel affecting the status of the city of Jerusalem, the United Nations reaffirmed these resolutions and the established principle that acquisition of territory by military conquest is inadmissible. It deplored the failure of Israel to implement the Security Council resolutions, censured Israel, declared the Israeli actions concerning the Old City invalid, and called on Israel to rescind them. Israel simply rejected these resolutions as interference in her sovereignty and decided that the only answer was to settle thousands of Jews in East Jerusalem and the surrounding hills. Rabbi Itzhak Nissim, Sephardi Chief Rabbi, declared that the resolution defied divine prophecies. Israel did make an offer to the United Nations on October 8, 1968, to place the Christian and Muslim holy places in Jerusalem under the responsibility of "those who hold them in reverence."

The Land of Israel Movement feels strongly that every inch of territory should be kept, because this is "the inherent and inalienable rights of our people from the beginnings of its history." The West Bank is referred to as "the very heart of our homeland . . . withdrawal from Judea and Samaria would jeopardize the very existence of Israel and its population." Again and again the movement speaks of "the inherent claim of the Jewish people to the whole land of Israel" of the "inherent and inalienable connection between the people of Israel and the land of Israel." A strong plea is made to settle Jews in the new areas. According to the Land of Israel Movement, the Jewish nation is linked to the land and the soldiers of Israel in 1967 did not fight on foreign soil as did, for instance, the Russian armies in 1944. Yet as a result of the war with Germany and Japan, Russia annexed to itself one-third of a million square miles of additional territory and additional populations numbering 22½ millions. These annexations were recognized by the West, including the United States. Yugoslavia annexed territories from Italy, and Poland obtained East Silesia. All these arrangements have been recognized as politically and ethically justified yet Israel's claim to the territories — incomparably more justified — is not recognized. The territories are not annexed nor is it right to speak of expansion but rather of liberated territories.

In answer to the question "What are the boundaries of

the land of Israel?" the Movement answers that at different times Israel included parts of present-day Syria and Lebanon and of the Sinai peninsula. In fact, the Golan Heights, Sinai, and Transjordan all figured in Zionist colonization projects at the turn of the century. In other words, the plea is made on behalf of the Land of Israel Movement that it carries out the original Zionist concepts. The conclusion is reached that "the Jewish right to the land of Israel is grounded in history, sanctified by tradition and sacrifice and finally reaffirmed in the modern law of nations." Over against this is the Arab viewpoint, perhaps best summed up by Henry Cattan who writes, "If justice is to be done in Palestine and peace to be restored in the Middle East, the clock must be turned back. In a somewhat similar situation in Algeria, where French immigrants implanted themselves in a land which was not theirs, the factual situation was undone after well over a century. The *fait accompli* — on which Israel has until now rested its existence, its policy, and its territorial conquests — cannot be accepted as a lasting situation or as a source of title in international relations. The Palestine injustice cannot be buried under a fait accompli."[15]

It is hardly necessary to underscore the obvious fact that Israeli and Arab viewpoints are diametrically opposed and no solution is in sight. The problem of the occupied territories cannot be solved aside from the refugee problem, and a general peace settlement in the area.

THE ARMS RACE

In recent years an unbelievable quantity of war matériel has been shipped to the Middle East by different arms suppliers. It is well known that Russia has refurbished the Arab military machine at a cost of at least one billion dollars. Only one year after the Six-Day War, Egypt announced a new strategy of "preventive defense," which simply meant that the UAR would launch offensive operations. More recently the USSR airlifted antiaircraft weapons to Egypt, to bolster Cairo's defense against Israeli air attacks.

At one point Western Germany played a significant role in providing arms to Israel. The news leaked out in 1965. Recently Switzerland got involved inasmuch as a Swiss aircraft engineer sold top secret Mirage jet engine blueprints to Israeli agents.

Great Britain has played a minor role. While the country debated the sale of Centurion tanks to Libya, France sold more than one hundred war planes to Libya, totally upsetting the delicate arms balance. For about a decade France had been the principal arms supplier of Israel. A total reversal of policy was probably dictated by the desire to gain renewed influence in North Africa, Libyan oil, a promise from Libya not to support rebels in the Chad, and the enormous economic advantage of the sale. The détente between the super powers which followed the Cuban crisis was a matter of concern to the Arabs because it weakened their bargaining position. They turned to France which, under De Gaulle, was anxious to play a significant part in the Middle East.

The arms deal with Libya came as a surprise. It is true that the United States had sent ten F-5 Freedom Fighters to Libya, but this was under the regime of King Idris and not to the new revolutionary government. One hundred planes are hardly necessary for Libyan security. In this connection it should be remembered that Egypt is unable to train enough pilots to fly the 350 Soviet aircraft in her possession. Libya with a more backward and smaller population will have a tough time learning to handle the French planes. In other words, the balance will not be upset in the immediate future. The French have sent instructors to Libya, which has greatly upset the Israeli government. Actually, the planes are to be delivered between 1971 and 1974. The uproar about the planes has almost eclipsed the sale of 200 tanks to Libya. Iraq has also received 200 tons of arms from France.

The United States has furnished arms to Jordan and Israel. The latter keeps asking for more and more but the United States tries to maintain a certain arms balance. The sale of French planes to Libya may force the United States to sell more Phantom jets to Israel to maintain the precarious arms equilibrium.

The United States has been accused of shipping arms to Israel from Germany via Belgium. Marked "scrap for Italy," the real destination appears to have been Israel. In the round of accusations and denials, it is at times difficult to know what the real situation is. The United States furnishes arms to Morocco, Saudi Arabia, Tunisia, Jordan, and Israel.

Israel is developing her own weapons. She now assembles the Fouga Magister trainer and has opened a jet engine plant at Bet Shemesh. The French Md-660 missile is produced in Israel. It can deliver more than 1000 pounds of high explosives as far away as Cairo or Damascus* Perhaps nuclear bombs, similar to those dropped on Hiroshima, have been produced in Dimona. According to Israeli sources the plant is used for peaceful purposes only. Inspectors found no evidence of a separation plant to produce the necessary plutonium. Of course, enriched uranium may have been purchased in France in years gone by or obtained from South Africa or Argentina.

The Israeli navy has not been distinguished in the past but the addition of French gunboats infused new life and power. Gunboats had been ordered from France and seven had reached Israel. The five remaining gunboats had been ordered by Israel before the French arms embargo (January 1969). The five boats have a French hull, German engines, and Italian electronics, including a twenty-mile surface-to-surface missile. The gunboats, or more properly missile boats, are small, 240-ton and 148 feet long. The UAR has twenty Soviet-built gunboats of the *Osa* and *Komar* classes. One of them sank the destroyer *Elath* with a Styx missile.

Israel acquired a significant quantity of weapons in the Six-Day War. More recently a commando unit attacked an Egyptian base 180 miles south of Suez and returned with a brand-new Soviet-made radar station. The seven-ton mobile unit was taken apart and brought back seventeen miles across the Gulf by helicopter. It was the first P-12 radar unit (used in conjunction with SAM-2 surface-to-air missiles and effective against low-flying aircraft) to fall into foreign hands in working order.

When Israeli commando units seized an isle in the Red Sea, the maritime radar unit located on the southern tip of Shadwan was taken intact.

Israel relies heavily on the excellence of her armed forces. Between 1936 and 1939 for all practical purposes a clandestine Jewish army existed. Many Jews fought with

---

*The only significant city within reach of Egyptian shells is Tiberius.

the allies in World War II and received excellent training. In May of 1941, the Palmach, a commando force, was created. It was an elite professional corps, the first full-time professional military unit of the Haganah. The Haganah, as an organization, came into being on June 25, 1921. By 1945 the membership was 45,000 or 7 percent of the population. They had only 700 trained officers. At the time, the Palmach numbered 2,000 and was the only combat-ready, full-time, professional unit.

The Israeli standing army is no larger than 80,000 men, but one-seventh of the total Jewish population is in the active military reserve. Some of the strongest leadership comes from the kibbutzim. In the Six-Day War, 25 percent of the total killed and wounded officers were from collective settlements which contain only 4 percent of the population. One of the great assets of the Israeli army is the youthfulness of commanders and senior officers. Chief of Staff and Brigadiers are in their forties, many Colonels in their thirties. Officers may serve until the age of 55 but in practice most of the senior commanders leave the army earlier.

Large sums of money are devoured by the arms race in the Middle East. In 1964, Iraq spent 10.9 percent of the gross national product on defense outlays and 12.2 percent in 1965. In Jordan the figure varied from 14.9 percent to 11.7 percent of the GNP between 1963 and 1965. Egypt has seen a steady increase over the last decade, moving from 5.7 percent of the GNP in 1954-55 to 12.2 percent in 1964-65. Lebanon, relatively quiet, has spent much less, but Syria allocated over 10 percent of the GNP for defense outlays. Israel followed the same course and reached a high of 12.2 percent of the GNP in 1966.* As a matter of fact, Egypt, Israel, Jordan, Iraq, Saudi Arabia, and Syria spent higher percentages of the GNP on defense during 1964

---

*Currently almost 20 percent of Israel's GNP is spent on defense or 40 percent of its current budget.

than any other countries in the world except the USSR. What this means in terms of economics, inflation, and living standard is beyond measurement.

Every year the London Institute for Strategic Studies publishes a report regarding the relative strength of the armed forces. The latest report pits 400,000 men under arms from the UAR, Jordan, Syria, and Iraq against 290,000 for Israel. In 1968 the figures were 353,000 against 255,000. The Arab countries have 2,200 tanks (only 1,940 in 1968) compared with 1000 for Israel (800 in 1968). Again, the Arab nations have 645 jet interceptors and fighter bombers (68 bombers and 889 fighters in 1968), whereas Israel has only 195 fighter bombers (15 bombers and 273 fighters in 1968). Egypt has the latest in equipment from the USSR, including Mig-21's, surface-to-air missiles and T-55 tanks. In spite of this, Israel has abandoned the concept of retaliatory raids and speaks of anticipatory counterattacks. The Egyptian euphemism of "preventive defense" and the Israeli slogan of "anticipatory counterattacks" can hardly veil the fact that Jews and Arabs are waging an aggressive warfare. Seldom, if ever, has there been such an accumulation of arms in a specific area without ultimately being used. War in the Middle East is only a matter of time. It has been said that the Arabs cannot win the war and the Israelis cannot win the peace. This impasse will not be solved by another war, but the armed conflict appears to be inevitable.

On the average, Middle Eastern countries have spent 12.8 percent of the GNP on armament over the last twenty years. The short-term trend has even been higher. From 1965 through 1968, the countries in that area have spent 19.9 percent of the GNP. It comes to $2.7 billion for the single year of 1968. The arms race is really pointless. It was in 1963 that the UAR obtained long-range surface-to-air missiles, but the same year they were also purchased by Iraq and Israel. Saudi Arabia followed in 1966 and Syria in 1967. These huge expenditures are made by countries which can least afford it. The main responsibility rests with the suppliers who either for political reasons (USSR and the United States) or economic gain (Great Britain and France) have continued to sell arms to the Middle East. Although these nations are meeting in an endeavor to find a formula for peace, they would help the situation immensely if they were to interrupt this enormous flow of military equipment to the Middle East. An arms control treaty concerning the Middle East would certainly be the first step toward peace. It has been objected that such treaties are worthless, but in reality there are now three arms control treaties affecting both the United States and the USSR: the demilitarization of Antarctica, the ban on nuclear weapons in outer space, and the partial test ban. These treaties have been effective.

It seems hypocritical on the part of the great powers to continue conversations about peace, sign U.N. resolutions to that effect, and yet at the same time furnish immense quantity of arms to the Middle East. Ultimately, arms will be used simply because they are available and because they seem — quite erroneously — to point to a solution. Since a military solution of the Middle East conflict is inconceivable, an arms limitation would be the first step toward reduction of tension.

RECONSTRUCTION OF THE TEMPLE

THE TEMPLE

In one of his letters the apostle Paul speaks of the son of perdition, the antichrist "who opposes and exalts himself against every so-called god or object of worship, so that he takes his seat in the temple of God, proclaiming himself to be God" (2 Thess. 2:4).

Some of the early church fathers expected a literal fulfillment. Irenaeus (A.D. 120-202) wrote: "When this Antichrist shall have devastated all things in the world, he will reign for three years and six months and sit in the Temple of Jerusalem" (*Against Heresies,* Book V, chap. 30, par. 4). Since by that time the Temple of Jerusalem had already been destroyed, Irenaeus must have expected the reconstruction of the Temple.

Chrysostom (A.D. 347-407), writing a little later, takes a different view. He explains that the antichrist "will be seated in the Temple of God, not that in Jerusalem only but also in every church" (in loco).

Paul sometimes uses the word Temple figuratively to describe the Church of Christ: Ephesians 2:21; 1 Corinthians 6:19; 2 Corinthians 6:16. The exact meaning of the text would have to be determined by the context. Several considerations add weight to the literal viewpoint:

—He *sits,* or takes his seat in the Temple of God;

—The usage of the definite article, *the* Temple of God;

—The definite relationship and dependence of the entire passage on Daniel 11:36;

—The possible relationship with Matthew 24:15 and Mark 13:14; in this last passage the masculine participle may indicate a person rather than an image;

—The possible relationship with Daniel 12:11.

For these reasons the literal interpretation is maintained by DeWette, Lünemann, Wieseler, Döllinger, and Milligan, to mention a few.

Augustine took an intermediate position: "It is uncertain in what Temple he will sit, whether in that ruin of the Temple which was built by Solomon, or in the Church. For the apostle would not call the temple of any idol or demon the Temple of God. And on this account some think that in this passage Antichrist means not himself alone, but his whole body, that is, the mass of men who adhere to him, along with him their prince; and they also think that we should render the Greek more exactly were we to read, not 'in the Temple of God,' but 'for' or 'as the Temple of God,' as if he himself were the Temple of God, the Church."

The argument of Augustine that Paul would not call the temple of any idol or demon the Temple of God is used by H. A. W. Meyer to accentuate Irenaeus' position: "On account of the definite expression 'sit' it cannot be otherwise understood than in its *proper* sense. But on account of the repetition of the article can only *one definite Temple* of *one definite true God* — that is, the Temple of Jerusalem — be meant" (in loco).

If many Christians expect a literal fulfillment of 2 Thess. 2 and wait for the reconstruction of the Temple, what is the Jewish view?

JEWISH VIEWPOINTS

It was the general opinion of the Rabbis that the Temple would be rebuilt in the days of Messiah and that all the sacrifices would be reinstituted at that time. Occasionally there was a dissenting voice. In the Midrash a tradition is quoted, indicating that "all sacrifice will cease in the future, except the sacrifice of praise and thanksgiving, even as it is written: 'both companies of those who gave thanks stood in the house of God' (Neh. 12:40)."

The Jewish prayer book is full of aspiration and longing for the reconstruction of the Temple, but whether most Jews, be they religious or non-religious, would really be anxious to see the entire ritual restored is questionable. The basic content of the prayer book dates from a period shortly after the destruction of the Temple in A.D. 70 when the memory of the glorious ritual was still fresh in the minds of many and the yearning deep and serious. More recently, non-orthodox Jewish groups have deleted references to the rebuilding of the Temple from their prayer books.

When the Emperor Julian the Apostate offered to rebuild the Temple in the fourth century, Jewish response was anything but enthusiastic. It was more interesting to discuss problems abstractly or to discover mystical meaning, to define the exact measurements and the architectural layout of the sanctuary and of the surrounding buildings, to describe the furniture, the vessels, the vestments and the ritual, than to reconstruct the Temple.

It is surprising that the reconstruction of the Temple was seldom discussed by Rabbis across the centuries. One notable exception was R. Kalischer, a strenuous advocate of resuming the sacrificial rites.

Problem 1:

Although it is true that a great amount of detail regarding topography and ritual is found in the Talmud and was later codified by the famous Maimonides (1135-1204), the exact interpretation of these statements is uncertain.

Solution:

The sacrificial ritual could be resumed without the Temple. When the Jews returned from the Babylonian exile "they built the altar of the God of Israel, to offer burnt offerings upon it" (Ezra 3:2) long before the Temple was rebuilt. To this Maimonides agrees. Knowledge of the place where the Temple stood and access to or possession of the site are the only necessary prerequisites.

Problem 2:

The Temple area may only be approached in a state of ritual purity. Practically every Jew lives in a state of ritual defilement since everybody has at one time or another been in contact with a dead body, visited a cemetery, etc. Cf. Num. 19:11 ff. In order to obtain levitical purity the ashes of a red heifer mixed with water have to be sprinkled on the unclean person (Num. 19). For this reason orthodox Jews never set foot on the Temple area. The site is legally inaccessible. Jews can pray at the Wailing Wall because it is the *outer* wall of the Temple area.

Solution:

The sanctity of the site has been challenged. Some Jewish scholars have maintained that with the destruction of the Temple, all sanctity vanished from the site. Consequently prohibitions concerning ritual impurity are no longer in effect. The holiness with which the site was invested did not have an indelible character but disappeared along with the temple in A.D. 70.

Problem 3:

Still in the area of levitical purity, it has been pointed out that no one could perform the sacrifices since all have been defiled.

Solution:

R. Kalischer answered years ago by pointing to a talmudic rule which stipulates that public sacrifices (for instance the morning and evening burnt offerings) suspend the rules of levitical defilement.

Problem 4:

Only members of the family of Aaron can perform the holy rites and it is difficult — if not impossible — to determine who descended from Aaron.

Solution:

A certain tradition has been handed down, sufficient at least for the synagogue ceremonial. Only a descendant of Aaron can give the priestly benediction in the synagogue service. Although the evidence may not be airtight, the tradition (accepted for the synagogue ritual) may be deemed sufficiently reliable to permit service in the Temple.

If orthodox Jews have shown extreme reluctance and liberal Jews a slight touch of horror when the reconstruction of the Temple or the resumption of sacrifices are mentioned, the situation may change drastically since the events of 1967. The Old City of Jerusalem and the Temple area are once again in Jewish hands, almost compelling a rethinking of the situation.

In the end the chief consideration regarding the rebuilding of the Temple may not even be religious but nationalistic. Would such a building not give renewed expression to Jewish consciousness, serve as a symbol of spiritual unity, and be a focal center for Jewry worldwide? The feeling that the Temple will be erected in the days of Messiah may yield to political pressure. In the past it had also been taught that the return to the land would have to wait for the coming of Messiah. Here too, political considerations overruled religious sentiment and the same might happen regarding the building of the Temple.

From time to time a lone voice is heard urging the rebuilding of the Temple. In 1967, R. Lehiman quoted R. Hisda who said that the world had not witnessed the true radiance of the sun in a perfectly clear sky since the destruction of the Temple. No reference was made by the Rabbi to sacrifices or to the priestly order, since they were not mentioned in Solomon's prayer of dedication nor viewed favorably by the prophets. This appeal was reminiscent of the words of R. Akiba who hoped to rebuild the Temple to strengthen the revolt of Bar Kochba against the Romans.

It is not politically expedient to discuss such matters in the Jewish press since the Temple site is occupied by the Mosque of Omar. It is true that an act of God could change the situation instantaneously. An earthquake could dispose of the Mosque. The fire which damaged the Aksa Mosque (set by a non-Jewish religious fanatic) could have spread to the Mosque of Omar, immediately adjacent, and destroy this Muslim sanctuary. Since doubt has been expressed from time to time regarding the ability of the Jews to protect the "holy places," Jewish people have been extremely careful to avoid discussion of a possible reconstruction of the Temple. Incidentally, why Jews should be less able to guard the so-called Christian holy places than the Muslims is a mystery. That churches, mosques, and synagogues have been damaged by Jews is to be expected in time of war. For that matter, Arabs destroyed or damaged eighty places of Jewish worship when they controlled Jerusalem, turning two synagogues into public lavatories (*Time,* June 27, 1969).

NEW LOCATION

But in all these discussions regarding the Temple something else has been overlooked. Although the reconstruction of the sanctuary is indicated in 2 Thessalonians, the exact location is not. Most Jews and Christians seem to take for granted that the ancient site is the only possible one. The opinion of some rabbis that the sanctity of the place vanished with the destruction of the Temple has already been mentioned. In fact, the Bible speaks of another possible location.

It is difficult to interpret the last eight chapters of Eze-

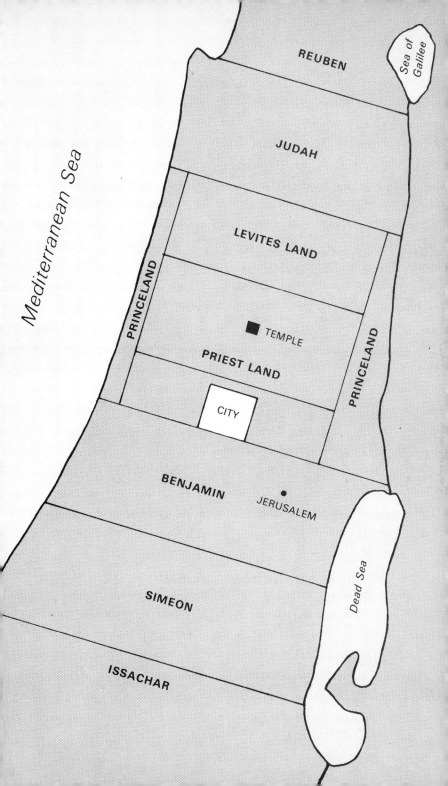

kiel, but regardless of the view which is taken, one idea stands out quite clearly: the Temple envisaged by Ezekiel was not located in Jerusalem. At this point the question whether this temple should have been built after the exile, later in history (or during the tribulation?), in the millennium, or whether the idea was symbolic, is immaterial. The principle remains that a holy Temple could be built elsewhere than in Jerusalem. The sanctuary was to be in the territory between Judah and Benjamin, in a holy district reserved for the priests, the Levites, and the prince. The portion of the land set apart for holy purposes was equal to a normal tribal portion. The Levites were to occupy the area next to Judah (north), the priests the heartland, the city was to be south of the most holy portion, and the sides of the district were reserved for the prince. As might be expected, the Temple was in the center of the priestly portion (Ezek. 48:8 ff.; 45:1-8). Not that Ezekiel is necessarily predicting how and where the Temple to be occupied by the antichrist shall be built, but he certainly indicates that a holy temple could be erected in some other place than the ancient threshing floor of Araunah, a site currently occupied by the Mosque of Omar.

If a temple should exist during the millennium (Ezek. 37:26-28), what the purpose might be and where it would be located are related questions. That the antichrist will pitch his palatial tents "between the sea and the glorious holy mountain" (Dan. 11:45) is a slight indirect confirmation of 2 Thessalonians 2. Somewhere between the sea (the Mediterranean Sea) and the glorious mountain (Mount Zion) antichrist will establish himself and "come to his end, with none to help him" (Dan. 11:45), when "the Lord Jesus Christ will slay him with the breath of his mouth and destroy him by his appearing and his coming" (2 Thess. 2:8b).*

---

*For additional notes concerning the antichrist see the author's *Contemporary Commentary on Thessalonians*: Appendix I The Antichrist, published by Tyndale House Publishers.

Embedded in Jewish tradition is the saying that all the prophets spoke only of the coming of Messiah. Some Rabbis recognized that the Messiah is the heart and center of the Old Testament revelation. As might be expected, speculation concerning the coming and ministry of Messiah abounded. It was precisely because of definite eschatological expectations on the part of the scribes and Pharisees that they rejected Jesus who did not conform to their theological presuppositions. It was always dangerous to adhere rigidly to a prophetic program to the point of failing to understand God's action. Christians are subject to the same temptation.

It is of particular interest to Christians to read about ancient — and still valid — rabbinical speculations concerning the coming of Messiah. If some of these ideas evoke mild surprise it must not be forgotten that they were presumably based on the Old Testament. Even though Christians have the New Testament revelation they too may entertain many outlandish notions regarding prophecy. This has certainly been true in the past and even today many divergent views prevail in the church.

EVENTS PRECEDING
THE COMING OF THE MESSIAH

According to ancient Jewish tradition, ten events will announce and precede the coming of Messiah.

1. God will allow three masters in seduction to deceive the whole world. They will easily blind and seduce mankind so that all nations and even many Jews will become irreligious and despair of the coming of Messiah. Believers will hide out in caves and the world will be devoid of defenders of truth. The children of Israel will remain for a long time without prince, without king, without sacrifices, and without altar. Heaven will be like brass and famine will prevail. Through the cruelty of these three rulers the misery of mankind will reach the highest pitch. In the end these kings will suppress all worship of God and impose a ten-fold tribute upon the Jews. Whoever refuses to pay will be beheaded. After nine months, people with two heads, with fiery and blood-red eyes, and feet faster than the speed of deer will invade (the world or Israel?). No one will resist and the fear of death will grip everyone. The streets will be full of crying infants and screaming adults.

2. God will allow the sun to come so close to the earth that the heat will be unbearable and produce insanity, fever, pestilence, and sickness. Men everywhere will fall to

the ground by the thousands and die. They will scream: "Where shall we flee?" Many will dig their own graves and others will hide in holes and clefts of the rock. The Jews will have a balm against this scorching ray of the sun. So Mal. 4:2 will be fulfilled.

3. God will allow a bloody dew to fall which will be like deadly poison for all the Gentiles and Jews who have not believed in the coming of Messiah. The godly will not be hurt. This dew will cover the earth for three days and the earth will appear bloody (Joel 2:30).

4. God will allow a healing dew to fall, destroying the bloody dew. This dew will heal the lukewarm who had become sick from the poisonous dew (Hosea 14:5).

5. According to Joel 2:31, darkness will cover the earth for thirty days. Then the sun will return to her previous splendor. The nations will recognize that this sign occurs because of Israel and they will be ashamed and fearful. Many will accept Judaism secretly.

6. God will allow the godless Edomites (Christianity is intended) to extend over the entire earth. In Rome a king will rise and control the whole earth for nine months. The Jews will feel his heavy hand. He will impose a tribute on them and they would despair if his rule were to continue. After nine months the Messiah, son of Joseph, will come whose name is Nehemiah ben Kushiel. Several tribes will return to Israel under his guidance. When those still exiled hear about this, they will come from the four corners of the earth to join the army of Messiah. He will battle the king of Edom, conquer and kill him, ravage the entire Roman empire, and obtain much booty — including the utensils of the Temple. He will return to Jerusalem, kill all the people between Damascus and Ascalon, and make peace with the king of Egypt.

7. From a marble statue in Rome shaped like a beautiful young maiden, created through the power of God, a monster will arise. Innumerable young people will have intercourse with this statue as if she were a living person

and the result of this unnatural relationship will be a creature of human form but unbelievable size. This monster will have two heads, hair of fiery color, deep-seated eyes separated by a considerable distance, and green feet. This is Armillus, the antichrist, who will tell the Edomites (i.e., Christians) that he is the Messiah. He will claim to be God. All will believe him and receive him as king. After conquering many nations he will ask for a copy of the New Testament and say: "The law which I have given you is truth. I am your Savior; believe in me."

He will send for Nehemiah son of Kushiel, and request obedience from him. The Messiah will appear with 30,000 powerful heroes and read Exodus 20:2, 3: "I am the Lord your God, you will have no other gods before me." In the ensuing battle between Armillus and the Messiah 200,000 men of Edom will fall. Armillus will retreat to the valley of Decision (Joel 3:14). Armillus will put the Jews to flight and kill the Messiah. However, he is ignorant of the fact that the Messiah has died because an angel will remove Messiah's body and bury him with Abraham, Isaac, and Jacob. The Jewish people will suffer terribly, not only because of Armillus, but even the archangel Michael will persecute them and diminish their number (Dan. 12:1). The few remaining righteous will hide in the wilderness and wait for the salvation of Israel. The fainthearted will say: "Is this the redemption for which we have hoped so long? Is he the Messiah who died like other men?" God will cleanse Israel like gold and silver (Zech. 13:9; Ezk. 20:38; Dan 12:10). The righteous will remain for forty-five days in the desert of Judah, and barely survive. Meanwhile, the godless Israelites will be killed. Armillus will fight and conquer Egypt and return against Jerusalem (Dan. 11:45).

8. The trumpet blast of the archangel Michael will be heard and effect the gathering of the scattered ones of Israel (Isa. 27:13; Zech. 9:14). Three times he will blow the trumpet. After the first time, the Messiah son of David will

appear accompanied by the prophet Elijah to comfort those who have waited for forty-five days in the desert. The same sound of the trumpet will terrify all the ungodly because it announces their imminent perdition. Pestilence and plagues begin.

Armillus, upset by the result of this trumpet call, gathers a new army to conquer Jerusalem and to fight the Messiah. God will not allow the Messiah to fight, but will say unto him: "Sit at my right hand," and to the Israelites, "Stand still and see the salvation of the Lord." God himself will fight (Zech. 14:3), and fire and brimstone will fall from Heaven (Ezek. 38:22). Armillus and his army (that is Christendom) who have destroyed the Temple will in turn be destroyed (Obd. 18).

9. The second trumpet call of Michael will open the graves around Jerusalem and God will call the dead back to life. The Messiah son of Joseph will be awakened by the Messiah son of David. The true Messiah will travel throughout all the nations to gather together the Jews who are still scattered. At his request the authorities will relieve them from service and kings and princes will carry them to Jerusalem on their shoulders.

10. After the third trumpet call of Michael, God will gather the ten tribes. This mighty army is surrounded by a cloud of glory and God himself will be their leader (Micah 2:13). The road which he travels to Paradise to celebrate the marriage feast of Messiah is lined with marvelous fruit trees so that none will hunger or suffer want (Isa. 41:18; 49:10). Other nations will not be able to take advantage of these blessings because immediately after the Israelites have passed, a flame of fire will destroy everything.

CONCLUSION

What are the chances for peace? Most peace proposals are unrealistic. Indeed, it is unlikely that any Israeli government would accept "great power guarantees." They have not been found reliable in the past. What would happen if Egypt were to impose another blockade? It is more prudent from the Israeli viewpoint to hold on to what they have and to keep the occupied territories. Recent elections in Israel indicate a hardening of the position.

In Israel the voters choose parties rather than individual candidates. The 120 seats of the Knesset or parliament are apportioned among the sixteen political parties according to percentages of the total vote. In the last elections, in October 1969, a total of 1,750,000 persons were eligible to vote (including 150,000 Arabs). More than 83 percent cast their ballots.

The result was an anticipated shift to the right. Mrs. Golda Meir formed a broad coalition government of twenty-four ministers (two more than the previous government). Thanks to the coalition the government is based on 102 of the Knesset's 120 members. The key persons aside from the Premier, Mrs. Golda Meir, are Yigal Allon, the Deputy Premier, and Moshe Dayan for the Defense, Abban Eban in Foreign Affairs and Ezer Weizman in Trans-

portation. Mr. Weizman is a flamboyant newcomer to Is-
raeli politics whose name in itself is a clarion call. Indeed,
Major General Ezer Weizman, former commander of the Is-
raeli air force, is the nephew of the late Chaim Weizman
(first President of Israel) and the brother-in-law of Moshe
Dayan. Sometimes described as a Jewish Jack Kennedy,
Weizman is known for his "hawkish" approach and fervent
Zionism.

It is difficult for the Israeli government to reach an agreement with Arab leaders. What guarantee is there that such
an agreement would be honored by future Arab leaders?
Considering the present turbulence and the many political
coups in the Arab world, it is difficult for Israel to place
much confidence in any agreement.

Meanwhile, Israeli military attacks continue. Their purpose is to bring the war to the outskirts of Cairo and to ex-
pose Nasser as a fraud. This might precipitate his downfall.
On the other hand, it could also work in a different direction.
It might generate a spirit of national patriotism and cohe-
sion in Egypt and create an adverse reaction from the one
anticipated in Israel.

Israeli attacks are also pursued as a natural answer to
armed provocation from the other side. This only increases
the danger of irrational response and increasing escalation.
Finally, military efforts are often for tactical reasons in order to prevent combat readiness of the enemy, thereby de-
laying the next round.

From the Arab viewpoint a conclusion of a peace treaty
with Israel does not seem to lie within the realm of possibility. Most Arabs stand firmly by the decisions of the Summit meeting held at Khartoum on September 1, 1967: No
recognition of Israel, no negotiation with Israel, and the re-
affirmation of the rights of Palestinians to their homeland.
Mr. Henry Cattan writes, "It should be clear by now to
anyone who understands the Middle Eastern situation that
any attempt to secure peace in the Middle East by means
which are based upon mediation, conciliation, negotiation or

agreement between the parties is unlikely to lead to any tangible results, because the differences between them are so extreme and profound that they cannot be bridged by any of the usual means for settlement of international disputes."[16]

The Arabs are committed to a war of attrition which, they feel, works in their favor. Mr. Safran points out that the Arabs have "discovered a new truth which has guided their position ever since. They learned that if hitherto in history peace had followed upon armistice, it was because of the implicit sanction held by the party that had proved stronger in the war to resume it and thereby impose greater evil upon the weaker party. Since in this case the party that had proved stronger was hamstrung by the United Nations and other powers and unlikely to apply the usual sanction, there was no need to go on from armistice to peace unless there were specific gains to be had from it. And the Arab government of the time saw little to gain and much to lose by making peace. . . . Though forced to sign armistice agreements that 'objectively' consecrated their failure, Arab leaders developed the rationalization that as long as they did not sign peace treaties, the game was not over yet. As Azzam pasha, then Secretary General of the Arab League, put it in an interview with a journalist: 'We have a secret weapon which we can use better than guns and machine guns, and this is time. As long as we do not make peace with the Zionists, the war is not over; and as long as the war is not over there is neither victor nor vanquished. As soon as we recognize the existence of the state of Israel, we admit by this act that we are vanquished.' "[17]

As someone put it recently, everyone expects the Arabs to be "fanatics," so that any real or apparent concession is welcomed with wonder and relief. At the same time the Jews are expected to be more reasonable, so that any intransigence on their part is regarded with special impatience (*Time,* Sept. 19, 1969). At this point, everything is distorted by deep-seated bitterness and mutual distrust. A peace treaty would be almost meaningless since it is difficult to conceive that the population can really live together harmoniously.

Recently the Israeli Army Chief of Staff told military correspondents that national policy is no longer based on retaliation but on "continuous military activity, countering war with war." In a similar vein, Nasser has spoken of "taking the battle initiative back into our hands." Mr. Dayan, addressing Defense Force Commanders, said: "The conflict between us and the Arabs is insoluble. The war is not over this hill or that river, but over the very existence of the Jewish State in the Middle East."

What then are the chances for peace? They are slim indeed. It is true that an arms embargo on the part of all suppliers of military hardware to the Middle East would be a significant step toward reduction of tension. In fact, the "disengagement" of the big powers would be useful since their international interests seldom coincide with the national and local interests of the governments concerned. However, this is wishful thinking because both the USSR and the United States have far too much at stake in the Middle East to abandon the area. After centuries of futile efforts the USSR has finally gained a strong position in the Middle East and the United States is not ready to write off the area which is significant both in terms of population, economy (oil), and military strategy. With a certain amount of good will, the refugee question could probably be settled. Undoubtedly many Palestinians would like to return to the land west of the Jordan River. They should be welcomed by the Israeli government. Others would prefer life under Arab governments and should be absorbed by the surrounding nations. Financial help could be forthcoming both from the international community, the Arab governments, and Israel. The territorial problem could yield to a formula for peace. Ideally a federated state or a bi-national state could come into being. Whether Israel is prepared to pay this price for peace is questionable. It will be difficult if not impossible for any Israeli government to initiate such courageous action. It would seem that in the long run Israel would have to come to terms with her neighbors and that such a formula would become increasingly acceptable.

For the Christian, it is essential to retain a genuine Christian perspective. In the heat of rhetoric and passionate emotion this is not easy. At this point it is hardly necessary to point out that both Israel and the Arab nations are at fault. One-sided condemnations or endorsements are not helpful. It is not necessary for the Christian to endorse every act of the Israeli government simply because the nation exists in harmony with God's sovereign purpose. Nor is it wise to identify with the Arab refugees to the point of condemning every Israeli action, violently siding with the Arabs. It is essential to retain a genuinely independent, Christian point of view not unduly influenced by presumed knowledge of God's secret purposes, nationalistic feelings (pro-United States, pro-United Kingdom, etc.), nor emotionally unbalanced by an overemphasis on the plight and misery of refugees. All these factors must become part of the Christian consideration but in isolation none of them can be the determining factor.

One immediate concern of the Christian is the situation of the Church in the Middle East. As Christians we should certainly favor anything which would tend to give additional freedom to the existing churches, be it in Arab nations or in Israel. The furtherance of the kingdom of God, the proclamation of the gospel of Jesus Christ is the primary interest of each and every Christian. Discrimination against Christians whether on the part of Israel or the Arab nations should be a matter of grave concern to believers everywhere. A concern for the refugees is certainly dictated by every Christian principle. This does not extend only to their material welfare but should be coupled with a spiritual concern. At the same time, it would not do to emphasize the spiritual to the exclusion of material help which is desperately needed. If an arms embargo could seriously further the cause of peace, then such action should be supported by Christians. In other words, whatever might effectively be done to stabilize the situation should be supported by Christians everywhere. At the same time, it is pointless to maintain illusions or utopian hopes. The entire history of mankind has been marked by wars and it is with specific reference to the Middle East and to the time of his return that Jesus said that there would be wars and rumors of wars and that nation would rise against nation and kingdom against kingdom. There will be wars — there will be other wars in the Middle East. It is precisely under such conditions, when people hope for peace in the midst of war, that anyone with a solid promise of peace will be well accepted. It is easy to see that a genuine peacemaker would receive the worship of the masses. Although this is true at all times, it is particularly true in an era of great tension and of repeated warfare. In this sense, the stage is set for the coming of antichrist with the promise of peace. However, the last word will be pronounced by the Prince of Peace who will slay the antichrist with the breath of his mouth and destroy him by his appearing. The grace of God has appeared already for the salvation of all men. Christians are now awaiting the appearing of the glory of our great God and Savior, Jesus Christ.

"Now when these things begin to take place, look up and raise your heads because your redemption is drawing near."

APPENDIX

RESOLUTION OF THE SECURITY COUNCIL S/RES/
242 (1967) OF NOVEMBER 22, 1967 CONCERNING
THE SITUATION IN THE MIDDLE EAST

The Security Council,

(1) *Expressing* its continuing concern with the grave situation in the Middle East,

(2) *Emphasizing* the inadmissibility of the acquisition of territory by war and the need to work for a just and lasting peace in which every State in the area can live in security,

(3) *Emphasizing further* that all Member States in their acceptance of the Charter of the United Nations have undertaken a commitment to act in accordance with Article 2 of the Charter,

1. *Affirms* that the fulfilment of Charter principles requires the establishment of a just and lasting peace in the Middle East which should include the application of both the following principles:

(I) Withdrawal of Israeli armed forces from territories occupied in the recent conflict;

(II) Termination of all claims or states of belligerency

and respect for and acknowledgement of the sovereignty, territorial integrity and political independence of every State in the area and their right to live in peace within secure and recognized boundaries free from threats or acts of force;

2. *Affirms further* the necessity

(A) For guaranteeing freedom of navigation through international waterways in the area;

(B) For achieving a just settlement of the refugee problem;

(C) For guaranteeing the territorial inviolability and political independence of every State in the area, through measures including the establishment of demilitarized zones;

3. *Requests* the Secretary-General to designate a special representative to proceed to the Middle East to establish and maintain contact with the States concerned in order to promote agreement and assist efforts to achieve a peaceful and accepted settlement in accordance with the provisions and principles in this resolution;

4. *Requests* the Secretary-General to report to the Security Council on the progress of the efforts of the special representative as soon as possible.

November 22, 1967.

NOTES

The Middle East (pages 7-11)

[1]The Department of State Bulletin. March 23. 1959.
[2]From *Israel's Fight for Survival* by Robert J. Donovan and the staff of the Los Angeles Times. Copyright © 1967 by the New American Library, Inc. By permission of the publisher.

Egypt (pages 25-38)

[3]F. Gardiner, *The Bible Commentary for Bible Students,* ed. Charles John Elicott (London: Marshall Brothers), in loco.
[4]Richard Wolff, *Israel Act III* (Wheaton, Ill.: Tyndale House Publishers, 1967), pp. 66-70.
[5]Gerald Sparrow, *The Sphinx Awakes* (London: Robert Hale Ltd., 1956), Appendix VI, "The Nasser Testament," p. 201.

Libya (pages 39-44)

[6]Wolff, *Israel Act III,* p. 76.
[7]"Our Defeat in Libya," *Chicago Tribune,* October 6, 1969. Reprinted, courtesy of the *Chicago Tribune.*

Sudan (pages 45-47)

[8]Rowland Oliver and J. D. Page, *A Short History of Africa* (Baltimore: Penguin Books, 1965), p. 39.
[9]Ibid.

Arab Unity (pages 75-77)

[10]Nadav Safran, *From War to War* (New York: Pegasus, 1969), p. 58.
[11]"Soviet Power in the Middle East," *Newsweek,* February 17, 1969, p. 46. Copyright Newsweek, Inc., 1969. Quoted by permission.

The Issues (pages 91-92)

   [12]*The Israel-Arab Reader,* ed. Walter Laqueur (New York: Bantam
      Books, 1969), article by I. F. Stone, p. 308. © 1967 by The
      New York Times Company. Reprinted by permission.
   [13]Ibid., article by Laqueur, "Is Peace in the Middle East Possible?",
      p. 368.
   [14]Ibid., p. 356.

Conclusion (pages 165-170)

   [15]Henry Cattan, *Palestine: The Arabs and Israel* (London: Long-
      mans, Green and Co. Ltd., 1969), p. 41.
   [16]Ibid., pp. 195, 196.
   [17]Safran, *From War to War,* pp. 37-39.